MODERN
CROSS STiTCH

MODERN
CROSS STITCH

OVER 30
FRESH AND NEW COUNTED
CROSS-STITCH PATTERNS

Hannah Sturrock

OF BOBO STITCH

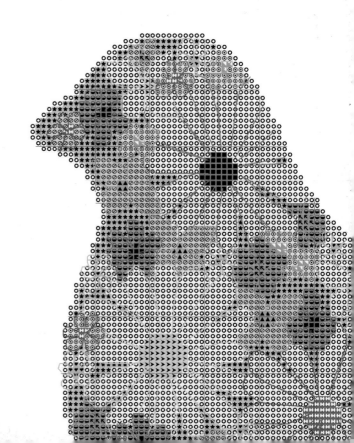

CICO BOOKS

LONDON NEW YORK

For James. It had to be you.

Published in 2015 by CICO Books
An imprint of Ryland Peters & Small Ltd
20–21 Jockey's Fields   341 E 116th St
London WC1R 4BW   New York, NY 10029
www.rylandpeters.com

10 9 8 7 6 5 4 3 2 1

Text and charts © Hannah Sturrock 2015
Design, photography, and illustrations © CICO
Books 2015

A CIP catalog record for this book is available
from the Library of Congress and the British
Library.

ISBN: 978 1 78249 240 5

Printed in China

Editor: Sarah Hoggett
Designer: Elizabeth Healey
Photographer: Jo Henderson
Stylist: Nel Haynes
Technique illustrator: Stephen Dew
Cross stitch charts: Hannah Sturrock

Senior editor: Carmel Edmonds
In-house designer: Fahema Khanam
Art director: Sally Powell
Head of production: Patricia Harrington
Publishing manager: Penny Craig
Publisher: Cindy Richards

CONTENTS

iNTRODUCTiON

I love to cross stitch. Really, truly, and passionately. This is a great comfort blanket of a hobby. You can do it in front of the television, listening to your favorite music, or just enjoying some peace and quiet. It's a good entry-level craft and, once you've mastered the basics, you can create some amazingly pretty things.

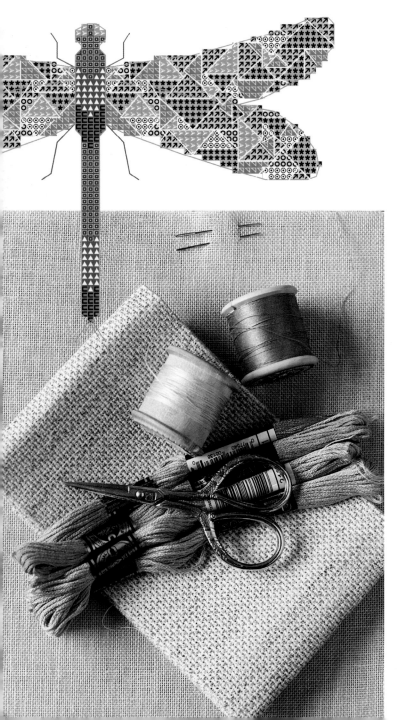

My only problem with cross stitch is that, for a long time, I didn't actually like a lot of it. Now don't get me wrong—this is not a judgment. There are millions of avid cross-stitch fans out there who love nothing more than to cross stitch a beautifully detailed historical sampler or a whole bundle of cute kittens, and they can't all be wrong. I simply mean it is not really my cup of tea. I stitched them, because I love to stitch— but then I didn't really know what to do with my finished projects.

When my nearest and dearest started to announce they were expecting babies, something came over me. I started wanting to make. To create something special. Something that would be treasured for generations. I didn't know how to knit, or crochet, or weave, or paint, or do those awesomely intricate paper-cut pictures. But I did know how to cross stitch. Remembering how much I loved to do it, I joyously began to search for the perfect pattern. Something stylish, using beautiful colors. And I searched. And I searched...

As with many small businesses, Bobo Stitch was born from a need: I couldn't find anything that wasn't cute puppies and fluff, so I made up my own patterns. I have no formal training, no art-school qualifications. But my friends liked my designs and so, little by little, I started selling contemporary cross-stitch kits. And here we are.

And now, oh boy—cross stitch is undergoing its own mini style revolution. A whole wealth of designers are creating beautiful, contemporary, complex designs in lots of different mediums. From beautiful life-like portraits and landscapes created directly from photographs to the subversive and slightly off-beat, cross stitch is now a diverse art form reflecting many styles and tastes.

This book gives you contemporary designs that use fresh colors and modern patterns. You'll find ideas to show you that you can cross stitch onto pretty much anything—gorgeous colored linen

and aidas, clothing, burlap (jute) shopping bags, phone cases, and even painted interior walls.

The book is full of stuff that I can't wait to frame and put up on the wall, or wrap carefully in beautiful tissue paper and present proudly to a friend as a gift. These are not the kind of projects that, when finished, will kick around in the bottom of your sewing basket, because you don't quite know what to do with them. You will want to show them off. You will be saying, "Look! Look at this. I made that."

A short while ago, I was selling some of my kits at a rather lovely craft fair. We had lots of customers who loved the designs, but every now and again you'd spot one. Another true addict. They stop. They stand. They stare. They run their fingers over the stitches. They think about how many projects they have yet to finish and whether they can squeeze in another one, because this one is just so pretty. I am always happy to spot a fellow avid stitcher, but I'm even more delighted to convert a newbie—so thread up, dive in, and let's see where you end up on the scale.

CROSS STITCH BASICS

Cross stitch is one of the easiest crafts out there—it's quick to learn and should provide instant gratification. The designs in this book are counted cross stitch, which means you stitch onto blank fabric following a pattern printed on paper.

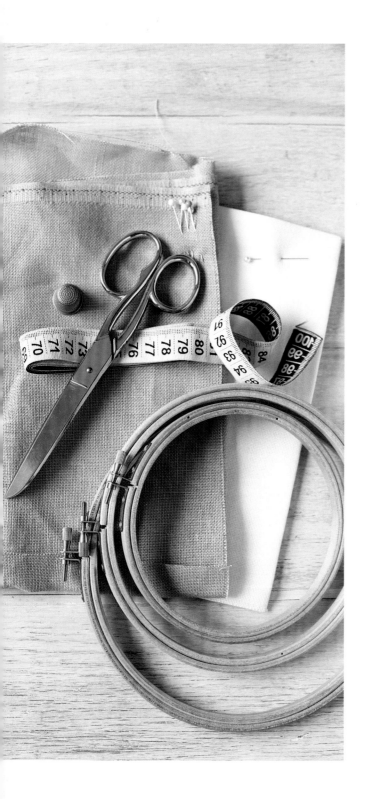

BASIC KIT

Before we begin, there are a few bits of basic kit that you will need—a bit like store-cupboard basics in a cookery book (although you won't need all of these for every project).

There are lots of other fancy bits of kit that you can buy, such as daylight bulbs to help you stitch into the night, frames (like an embroidery hoop but rectangular and bigger), stitch count markers, and so on. If you are a beginner there is no need to worry about this stuff. As you become more addicted, then add to your stash as you wish!

ESSENTIALS

- Small, sharp scissors for trimming floss (thread)
- Large scissors sharp enough to cleanly cut fabric
- Tape measure
- Cotton thread and a sharp needle for hand sewing
- Pins
- Ruler
- Pencil and eraser
- Iron and ironing board

HANDY BUT NOT ESSENTIAL

- Embroidery hoops—use them to keep your fabric at even tension while stitching, which can result in neater stitches. Choose one that has a diameter about 2 in. (5 cm) wider than the longest edge of your project, so that you don't have to keep moving it around.

- A sewing machine—great if you've got one, but all projects here can be easily finished by hand.

- A magnifying glass—this can make it easier to see the holes in the fabric, especially when using linen.

- A thimble and needle threader (see Top Tips on page 10).

EMBROIDERY FLOSS (THREAD)

Cross-stitch floss (or thread, as it is also known) is your ink to the fabric's paper. Throughout this book, DMC stranded floss is used—great quality, colorfast, and easy to source. It comes in 8¾-yd (8-meter) lengths bundled as six single threads together; this is called a "skein."

Occasionally I've thrown in a Kreinik thread for good measure. Kreinik make super metallic threads, which can add a beautiful shine to your embroidery. They are easy to use and available in lots of good craft stores. These come on a bobbin as a single thread. No need to separate here. Cut a slightly shorter length when using metallic threads, as they can fray and tangle more easily during stitching. Try about 12–14 in. (30–35 cm) instead.

Thread colors are given numbers—for example, DMC 943 is a very fetching shade of jade green. Each of the patterns has a key that tells you the thread numbers you will need to complete that design and a basic description of their color. Each pattern is totally customizable—if you are not keen on a particular color, then just substitute one you prefer. Easy!

Separating the strands

Often you will only need one or two of the six strands to stitch with. The number that you need for each color is clearly stated in the key chart that accompanies each of the patterns. Split the skein only as and when you are ready to use it.

1 Start by cutting about 20 in. (50 cm) from the skein. (Any shorter and you will be starting and stopping frequently. Any longer and you may get tangled.) Pinch the six strands together at the top.

2 Grab a single strand between the thumb and forefinger of your other hand and gently pull it upward—it will come loose. It will feel as if the remaining five strands have tangled themselves, but just straighten them out and repeat until you have the number of strands that you need.

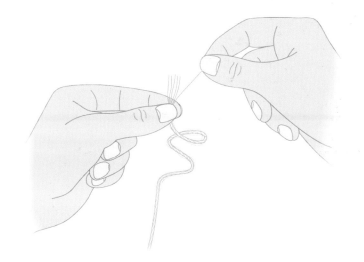

YOUR FABRIC

You can cross stitch onto anything that has holes arranged in an even grid. In this book there are patterns to cross stitch into woven chair bases, plastic punched phone covers, and wooden key rings. The thing to remember is that, whatever you are stitching onto, the basic principles of cross stitch are the same: you use the holes to guide your needle through the fabric to create your image. Common fabrics used in cross stitch are aida, even-weave, and linen. Aida is easier for beginners to get to grips with, but linen gives a finer finish.

Aida

Aida is woven with multiple threads in the grid. It is great for beginners, as each hole is easy to see. You simply use the four holes in each corner of one square on the grid to make one cross stitch.

Aida is described in "counts," which basically describes the number of cross stitches (or little Xs!) that fit into 1 in. (2.5 cm) both vertically or horizontally. The higher the count of the fabric, the smaller the stitches. The most common counts are 11, and 14, but it can go as low as 6 (for really big holes and stitches) or as high as 18 (for teeny, tiny stitches)!

You can make any of the patterns easier by stitching them onto larger aida (try 11-count, perhaps). Just remember that the finished piece will be bigger as a result of this.

Even-weave and linen

These fabrics are woven with a single thread to create the grid. They can be used to get very fine detail and have a smoother finish, giving your stitching a more refined look.

Generally, and in each pattern in this book, when using these fabrics you stitch "over two," using every other hole. So in this case nine holes (three up and three across) makes one square and one cross stitch.

Like aida, linen is also described in "counts"—but as you only stitch into every other hole, a 28-count linen gives the same size of stitches as a 14-count aida.

Water-soluble canvas

Soluble canvas is a great little invention that allows you to stitch onto fabrics that don't have an even grid, like cotton. This means the possibilities for cross stitch just got a lot bigger! It has a grid that is the same size as 14-count aida and is really easy to use. Take a look at our full instructions on page 16.

TOP TIPS

- When stitching "over two," always make stitches immediately next to ones that you have already done to avoid any counting errors.

- Buy a wire needle threader. They are very cheap and make threading needles easier, quicker, and less frustrating! Just push the thin wire loop through the eye of the needle (it fits through easily), then push your thread through the large hole in the wire loop, pull the wire back through the eye, and your thread goes with it.

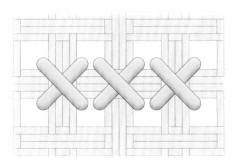

Three simple cross stitches on aida fabric, stitched into every hole.

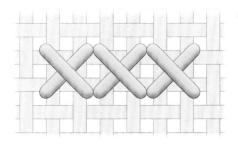

Three simple cross stitches on linen, stitched into every other hole.

NEEDLES

Each project in this book gives you the size and type of needle that you need to complete it.

Tapestry needles have a blunt tip and a large eye and are good to use on aida and even-weave fabric. Embroidery needles have a sharp tip and thin eye and are best used on other fabrics such as cotton, as they can pierce easily and leave a smaller hole.

Threading your needle

To thread your needle, loop the threads over the eye, pinch tight, slide the needle out from between your fingers, and push the pinched thread through the eye. Alternatively you can just push the ends of the thread through the eye directly, but do not lick it as it can damage the thread. You should pull a good 4–6-in. (10–15-cm) tail through the eye to stop you from losing the thread while stitching.

UNDERSTANDING YOUR PATTERN

The pattern is printed on a grid, which represents the fabric. Each color of floss (thread) has its own symbol, and one symbol in a square on the grid represents one cross stitch. See "Charted design" and "Stitched design" below. If there is no symbol in a square, there is no stitch there!

The key that accompanies each cross-stitch pattern—see "Thread color key" below—shows what symbol is used to represent each color of floss. It also tells you how many strands of that color to use for both cross stitch and backstitch or long stitch.

The pattern may be printed across several pages to make it easier to see. Where this occurs, there is an "overlap" section printed in gray to show where the

two sections join—don't stitch it twice! The center point of the design will also be marked on the pattern with intersecting lines, showing you the best place to start.

I have not included an average stitching time for any of the patterns. Instead there are two skill levels— one for the pattern and one for the material on which it is stitched. They are rated out of 5, with 1 being the easiest and 5 the most difficult. This way you can easily see from each of the patterns which ones will be quicker and which may take more love and attention. It's not a race and there's no reason to feel bad if you take a long time to stitch a piece. It's all about the process.

Charted design

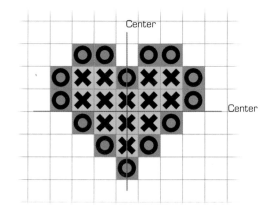

Stitched design

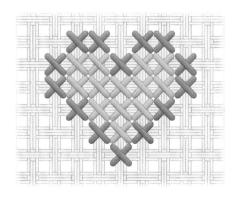

Thread color key

Symbol	DMC No	Description	Number of strands for cross stitch	Number of strands for long stitch
✖	964	Green	2	—
⊙	962	Pink	2	—

AND SO WE BEGIN...

Start in the middle! You can do this by folding your fabric in half both lengthwise and across the width. Where the four-way crease appears is the center of your fabric. If you cannot fold your fabric, then measure it to find the middle.

If you are using an embroidery hoop, now is the time to get it out. Separate the two hoops, lay the fabric over the bottom hoop, with the center point in the middle of the hoop. Place the top ring over the fabric and push it down onto the bottom ring. Pull the fabric taut and tighten the screw at the top until the fabric is held securely in place.

Find the center of the design on your pattern using the intersecting lines on the chart. Thread your needle with the color of the central stitch and get going!

To start, push your needle through one of the holes in the middle of the fabric and leave about a 1–1½-in. (3–4-cm) tail of thread behind the fabric. You will use this to anchor the floss to prevent it from coming loose later. Don't knot the end, as it makes everything too lumpy.

Cross stitch

Cross stitch is exactly as it sounds—two diagonal stitches that cross over each other to make an "X" shape. When you make the stitch, it doesn't matter whether the bottom stitch or the top stitch runs from bottom right to top left or vice versa, as long as you stick to whichever you prefer for the whole project.

Most people prefer to stitch row by row horizontally, but you can stitch from right to left, from left to right, or up and down. It doesn't matter.

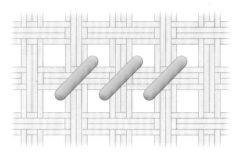

1 If you are working from left to right, count the number of cross stitches in your current floss color that there are from the center point. Make this number of diagonal stitches. (If they are left like this, these stitches are known as "half stitches.")

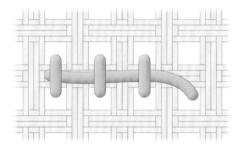

2 Turn the fabric over occasionally while making those first few stitches to make sure that you are catching the tail of the floss under the stitches to secure it.

xxxxxxxxxxxxxxxxxxxxxxxxxxxxxxxxxxxxxxxxxxxxxxx

TOP TIPS

• When using an embroidery hoop, position the screw at the top of your hoop diagonally opposite the hand you use to stitch, for example, top left if you stitch with your right hand. This will help to stop the thread from tangling on the screw fixings.

• If you make a mistake, don't worry. Use your needle to carefully unpick the stitches. The thread should be fine to reuse.

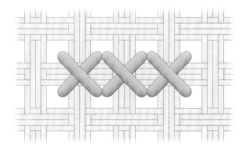

3 Then come back with the opposite diagonal. Not only have you completed some cross stitches, but you have produced some very neat stitches on the back of the fabric, too, which can be important if it is exposed to view.

WHERE NEXT?

A very common question from beginners is how to progress around the pattern. In reality, everyone will do this slightly differently. The more you stitch, the easier this will become. Don't worry too much if the back of your stitching looks a mess when you are starting out. It's the front that's important!

Having said that, I can show you the order in which I would tackle the example pattern. Generally I work in color blocks, doing one whole row of half stitches and then completing that row. Then I move up or down one row and repeat. Lots of experienced cross stitchers might shake their heads and tut at this, but as I said, everyone will do it differently.

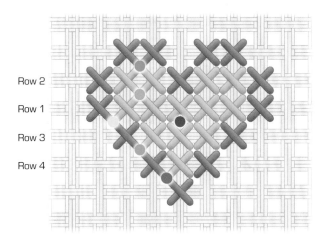

Row 2
Row 1
Row 3
Row 4

1 Start with your green floss. The red dot shows where the center of the pattern is. It is my preference to stitch whole rows in one go, so in this case, as the pattern is so small, you can easily count two squares to the left of the center square. To begin stitching, bring your needle up first in the hole shown by the yellow dot.

2 Make five half stitches (your bottom stitches) that run from the bottom left-hand corner to the top right-hand corner of each square, up to the end of the green section of row 1. Then come back, completing the crosses from right to left. You should now have five complete green cross stitches across the middle of the pattern.

3 Next, bring your needle up through the blue dot in the picture to begin row 2. Complete one half stitch (this time moving from top right to bottom left), then bring the needle up through the orange dot to do a second half stitch in the same way as before. Now skip a square (where you will ultimately make a pink

stitch) and do two more green half stitches. Come back from right to left and complete two crosses, skip that central pink square again, then complete the final two green cross stitches.

4 Now move down to complete row 3 by bringing your needle up through the hole marked with a green dot, do three half stitches from left to right, then three completed crosses from right to left.

5 And finally do the single stitch on row 4, starting by bringing your needle up through the purple dot. Now you've completed all of the green stitches, so secure the floss (see below).

6 Now thread your needle with two strands of the pink floss. Stitch individual complete crosses, starting with the single pink cross stitch in the center of row 2. Work clockwise around the heart to sew the remaining pink crosses.

Securing the thread

When you have finished a section, or if you are running out of floss, pass the needle under three or four stitches on the reverse of the fabric to catch and secure it in place. Remember, no knots are used in cross stitch. Cut off any excess floss close to the fabric.

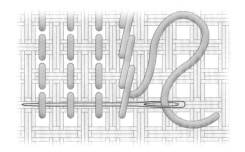

TOP TIP

In my designs, you will often find blocks of the same color that are separated by either blank fabric or another color. If these blocks are separated by more than three or four stitches, you should fasten off the floss securely, cutting and restarting for each block, rather than just stretching the thread along the back of the fabric. This prevents any kind of color "show through" or warping of the fabric.

OTHER STITCHES

So now you have mastered the basics, there are a few other stitches sprinkled among the pages of this book. I promise that they are used sparingly to give interesting definition or an awesome effect.

Backstitch and long stitch

These are both used to create definition and outlines. The techniques are described below. Your key will tell you which one to choose.

BACKSTITCH

Backstitch produces straight lines vertically, horizontally, or diagonally. Backstitches are short stitches across one square at a time. Backstitch is usually completed using only one thread. Where this is not the case, it will be marked on your pattern. Backstitch is indicated on your pattern with single straight lines.

Bring the needle up through the fabric at 1, make one straight stitch backward and take the needle down at 2, then pass the needle up through the fabric, two squares away forward, at 3, and go back down through the fabric at 4, through the hole where you originally came up for the first stitch at 1. In this way you progress around your outline, in a "two steps forward, one step backward" fashion. Don't pull these stitches too tightly, or you may distort your fabric.

LONG STITCH

This is a straight stitch that may go across several squares, starting or finishing either in one of the fabric's holes, or pushed through the aida, as happens with a three-quarter stitch. It is perfect for curved lines. The numbers in the illustration show where to position your needle.

Bring the needle up at point 1, down at point 2, and so on.

French knots

Having said that there are absolutely no knots in cross stitch, these ones are allowed—but they might take a little practice. They can be used to create dots for eyes, the center of flowers, and other general embellishments.

Bring your needle up through your fabric at the point where you want the knot to form. If you are right-handed, hold the needle in your right hand, use your left hand to keep the thread tight, and wrap it around the needle twice or more (the more times around, the bigger the knot). Pull the thread taut with your left hand so that the loops slip toward the point of the needle. Keeping that thread tight, push the needle back through the fabric just to the side of where you came up (so one square along on linen or through the weave of the aida). Pull through until your knot forms neatly on the front of the fabric.

Backstitch

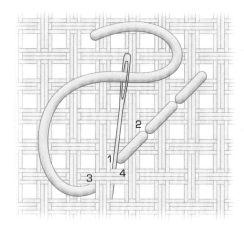

Long stitch

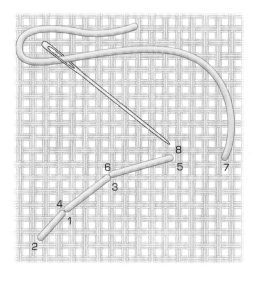

French knot

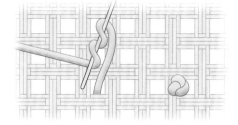

Three-quarter stitch

This can be used to add definition to a design where a full cross stitch would look too square. You stitch one half stitch and then a quarter stitch to create a triangle shape. The quarter stitch is begun as if you were going to complete a full cross stitch, but you stop halfway across and finish the stitch in the center of the X.

Three-quarter stitches can be stitched in four directions, as illustrated. On your pattern, three-quarter stitches are indicated by triangles that contain the correct color symbol. The direction of the triangle indicates the direction of the three-quarter stitch.

Three-quarter stitch

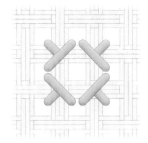

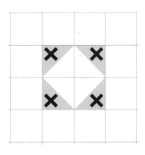

Three-quarter stitches worked on aida.

Three-quarter stitches as shown on a cross-stitch chart.

FINISHING

Once you have completed all the stitching, wash your finished article carefully by hand in cool water. DMC threads are colorfast and so will not bleed into each other or your fabric. Once washed, leave the article to dry on a flat surface. If it has become a little misshapen, then stretch gently back into shape and pin it to a cork board while it dries. Press between two clean dish towels while it is still a little damp.

CUSTOMIZE IT!

Remember that each pattern in this book can be stitched onto anything that has a grid—swap linen for aida, change colors, put the patterns created for the wall or phone case onto even-weave and frame them. It's your project, so make it as you want it—and most importantly, enjoy stitching it.

Now you are all set—so thread up and dive in!

DISPLAYING YOUR WORK

There are various ways you can display your finished pieces, from traditional frames and embroidery hoops to transferring your designs onto other fabric items. Here we explain the methods used in this book.

HOW TO USE SOLUBLE CANVAS

I love soluble canvas. It is so easy to use and means you can stitch onto practically anything. It is a slightly plasticky material that has an even grid of holes, giving the same size stitches as 14-count aida. You simply baste (tack) it onto your chosen fabric and stitch into the grid as normal. When you're done, wash the canvas away, leaving only your beautiful, perfect stitches behind. Instant gratification!

1 Wash and dry your fabric or garment and the two pieces of interfacing to ensure that they are pre-shrunk. Decide where on the fabric you would like your cross-stitched patch to be.

2 Iron your fabric or garment. Place one piece of interfacing, rough side down, on the reverse of your fabric where you would like the stitching to appear. This layer of interfacing helps to keep the fabric stable while you stitch. Place a clean, slightly damp dish towel over the top and press with a hot iron.

AFTERCARE

To protect your stitches, wash items separately on a cool wash and iron under a clean dish towel.

YOU WILL NEED

Your chosen fabric or garment

Two pieces of non-woven, iron-on (or fusible) interfacing slightly lighter than or the same weight as your fabric

Soluble canvas

Tape measure

Handsewing needle and cotton thread

Small sharp scissors

Iron and ironing board

3 Place the soluble canvas on the right side of your fabric or garment, where you would like the stitching to appear (this should be in the center of where you have just placed your interfacing on the reverse). Make sure your canvas is straight and exactly where you want it to be, then pin it carefully in place.

4 Thread your needle with a length of cotton thread in a contrasting color to your fabric. Run long stitches gently around the very edge of the canvas, so that the canvas, fabric, and interfacing are all caught in each stitch. Keep this stitch as close as possible to the edge of the canvas. Don't stretch the fabric while you are doing this, or your cross stitches will be distorted. Remove the pins.

5 Put your fabric in an embroidery hoop so that the whole of the canvas is visible and in the center of the hoop. Stitch the design, using the holes in the soluble canvas in the same way as you would onto normal aida. Don't pull your stitches too tight, as it will distort your fabric.

6 Once you have finished stitching, remove the hoop, then unpick all the long stitches from around the outside of the canvas. Snip away any excess canvas from the sides of the design, carefully avoiding your finished cross stitches.

7 Submerge your fabric or garment in hot water, taking care not to scald yourself, and leave it to soak for at least 10 minutes, preferably longer. Gently rub away any gooey residue left around the stitching area and then take the garment out of the water.

8 Lay your fabric out flat to dry. If, when dry, the stitched area looks shiny or stiff, simply repeat step 7.

9 Once dry, lay the second piece of interfacing rough side down over the back of the stitched area. (This piece of interfacing prevents the wearer of the clothes being irritated by your stitches.) Lay a damp dish towel over the top and press with a hot iron. Check that the interfacing is securely stuck.

10 You're all done!

5

6

HOW TO FRAME iN AN EMBROiDERY HOOP

Using an embroidery hoop is a quick, affordable, and effective way to frame your finished work.

xxxxxxxxxxxxxxxxxxxxxxxxxxxxxxxxxx

YOU WILL NEED

Finished piece of stitching

Embroidery hoop large enough to fit your finished piece

Acrylic paint

Small paintbrush

Iron and ironing board

Tailor's chalk or soft pencil

Non-fraying backing fabric (thin felt is great) slightly larger than your hoop

Fabric scissors

Sharp needle

Strong thread (for example, pearl cotton size 5)

Cotton thread

Small, sharp scissors

1 Separate the two rings of your hoop and paint the outer hoop in the desired color. (The inner hoop will be completely covered, so there is no need to paint this.) You might need a couple of coats. Leave the ring to dry for 24 hours, then carefully scrape off any paint you might have accidentally got on the metal hoop fastenings.

2 Take your beautiful, crease-free backing fabric (uh-oh, might have to get the iron out here). Using tailor's chalk or a soft pencil, lightly draw around the outer hoop ring on the reverse of the backing fabric. Cut out carefully and put to one side.

3 Position your finished, washed, and pressed cross-stitch piece over the inner hoop, then place the outer hoop on top. With the screw at the top, pull the fabric nice and taut. When you are happy, start screwing, stopping to tighten the fabric again after each half turn.

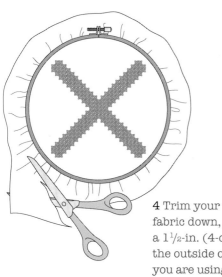

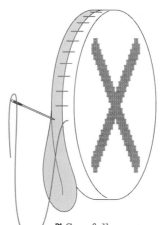

4 Trim your cross-stitched fabric down, leaving about a 1½-in. (4-cm) frill around the outside of the hoop. If you are using a 3-in. (7.5-cm) hoop, then leave only a ¾-in. (2-cm) frill.

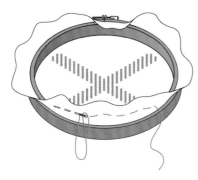

5 Thread your needle with a very long piece of strong thread. Starting at the bottom and leaving a tail of about 4 in. (10 cm), use running stitch to weave the thread in and out of your aida or linen about ¾ in. (2 cm) away from the hoop, all the way around; work your stitches about ⅜ in. (1 cm) away if you are using a 3-in. (7.5-cm) hoop.

6 When finished, pull the two tail ends of the thread downward to gather the fabric into the center of the hoop. Tie a tight knot to secure the thread ends together. Ask someone with clean hands to lend you a finger to assist here, as you really don't want to lose any tension while tying the knot.

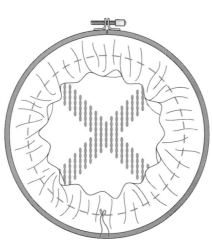

7 Carefully unscrew and remove the outer hoop. Center your backing-fabric circle around the inner hoop, so that it covers the back of your stitching. Thread your needle with cotton thread and use the simple over-and-over action of hemming stitch to attach the backing fabric to the cross-stitched piece at the side of the hoop, so that the stitches will be hidden when the outer ring is replaced. Make sure you keep the backing fabric taut and wrinkle free while you are stitching.

8 Replace the outer hoop and tighten the screw. Hang straight onto a nail or deep picture hook or tie a piece of ribbon onto the screw. Et voilà! Your piece is beautifully framed and ready to show off.

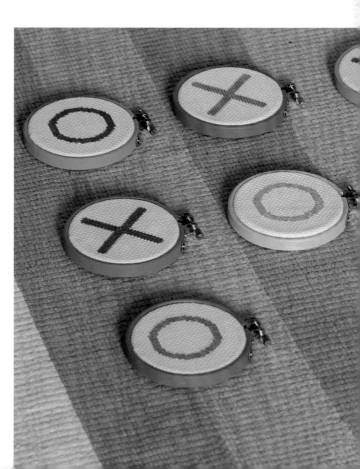

HOW TO MOUNT EMBROIDERY IN A PICTURE FRAME

The classic way to finish a piece of embroidery is in a gorgeous picture frame. If you follow the simple instructions below, there's no need to pay a fortune for professional framing.

xxxxxxxxxxxxxxxxxxxxxxxxxxxxxxxx

YOU WILL NEED

Finished piece of stitching

Picture frame large enough to fit your embroidery (make sure your fabric is at least 3–4 in. [8–10 cm] longer and wider than the frame)

Acid-free foam board or a piece of stiff cardstock

Pins

Strong thread (pearl cotton is ideal)

Sharp needle

Small, sharp scissors

1 Remove the wooden backing board from the frame, place it on the foam board, and draw all around it. Cut about ⅛ in. (2–3 mm) inside the drawn line all the way around, so that you end up with a piece of foam board just a tiny bit smaller than the inside of your frame.

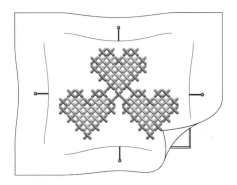

2 Place the foam board in the center of the back of your fabric, then pin the center of each side of the fabric to the edge of the board.

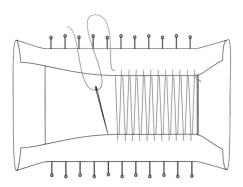

3 Pin all the way around each edge, making sure that the design is centered and the fabric is nice and taut, but not warped.

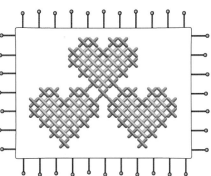

4 Thread your needle with strong thread and tie a knot in the end. Turn the board over and fold the top and bottom edges of the fabric down. Starting at the edge of the board, push the needle through the fabric about ½–¾ in. (1–2 cm) from the raw edge. Making sure the knot is holding securely, stitch back and forth from edge to edge, leaving about ⅜ in. (1 cm) between each stitch, until you reach the end of the foam board.

5 Flip over the board and check that the embroidery is still nice and central. Remove the pins from the top and bottom edges, then gently pull the stitches taut. Starting with the first stitch, pull each length of thread in turn, as you would with shoe laces, to tighten the thread; this in turn will pull the fabric nice and taut. Secure the thread by doing a few over-and-over stitches, or by tying another knot, but be sure not to lose any of that tension.

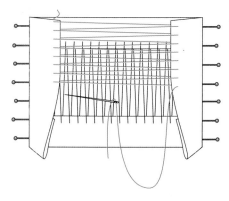

6 Fold in the two side edges, then repeat steps 4 and 5, this time with the stitches running across the board instead of up and down. Once finished, you should have a taut grid.

7 Now simply place your picture in the frame, replace the backing board, and hang it on the wall!

XXXXXXXXXXXXXXXXXXXXXXXXXXXXXXXXXXXXXXXX

TOP TIP

Choose a deep box frame, or remove the glass from your frame so that it does not press on and flatten your stitches.

HOW TO MAKE AN ENVELOPE PiLLOW COVER

This cover is simple and quick to sew, so there are no excuses for leaving any finished projects in the bottom of your sewing box. Finish it up and show it off!

XXXXXXXXXXXXXXXXXXXXXXXXXXXXXXXXXXXXXX

YOU WILL NEED

Finished piece of stitching

Two pieces of backing fabric cut to the size stated in the pattern

Plump pillow form (cushion pad) of the size stated in the pattern

Tape measure

Pins

Sewing machine if you have one; otherwise, a sharp needle with a small eye

Cotton thread

Small, sharp scissors

Fabric scissors

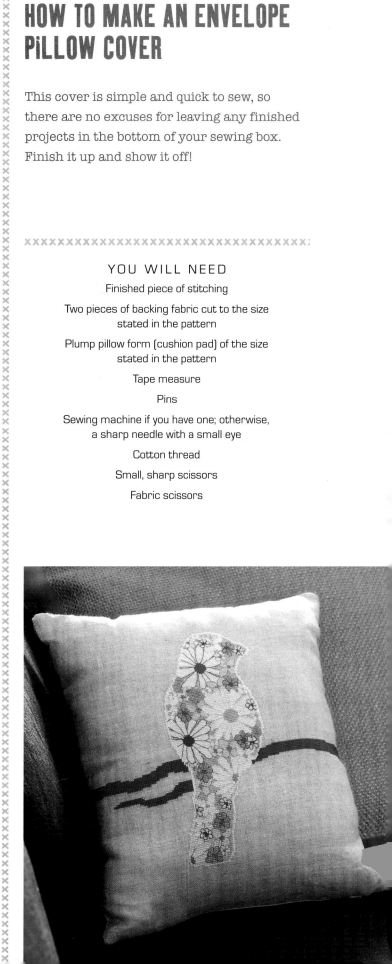

1 Wash and dry your stitching, following the instructions on page 15. Trim your cross stitch down to ³/₄ in. (2 cm) longer and ³/₄ in. (2 cm) wider than your finished cover size. For example, for a 14-in. (35-cm) cover, trim your stitching down to 14³/₄ x 14³/₄ in. (37 x 37 cm), taking care to keep your design in the center.

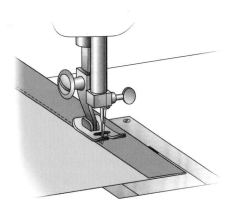

2 Wash, dry, and iron the two pieces of backing fabric to ensure that they are pre-shrunk. Press and pin a ³/₈-in. (1-cm) hem along one long edge of each piece of backing fabric for a square cover, then machine or hand stitch; for a rectangular cover, hem one short edge. (Note that the backing pieces for the Dachshund pillow on page 120 are actually square, so for that particular project, hem any edge.)

4 Place the second piece of backing fabric right side down over the top or left half of the cross stitch in the same way. The two pieces of backing fabric should now overlap in the center by about 3–4 in. (8–10 cm), with the hemmed edges in the middle. Pin all the way around the outside.

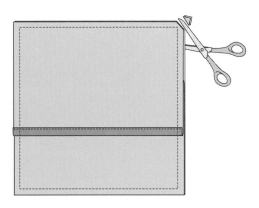

5 Stitch around the outside edge by hand or machine, taking a ³/₈-in. (1-cm) seam allowance all the way around. You can use the grid of the aida or linen as a guide to give you nice straight lines. Cut diagonally across each corner, taking care not to snip through your seam, so that your turned-out corners will be sharper.

6 Turn the cover right side out and push out the corners with a knitting needle or similar. Stuff with a nice fat pillow form (cushion pad) and voilà. Finished!

3 Place your cross-stitched piece right side up on a flat surface. Lay the first piece of backing fabric right side down on top, lining up the unhemmed bottom and side edges of the two pieces of fabric (or the right-hand side edges if you are making a rectangular pillow). Pin in place along the edge to hold the two pieces together.

XXXXXXXXXXXXXXXXXXXXXXXXXXXXXXXXXXXXX

TOP TIP

For rectangular pillows like our lovely Tartan Dachshund on page 120, your opening should run vertically down the back. Square pillows can have an opening that runs either vertically or horizontally.

HOW TO MAKE A DRAWSTRiNG SACK

These are instructions to make a basic drawstring sack, like the Christmas Sack on page 70.

1 When you have attached your finished cross-stitch design onto the fabric for the sack (see page 73), turn it over so you are looking at the wrong side. Fold the top (short) edge over by $^3/_8$ in. (1 cm) and press to give a firm crease to hide the rough edge. Fold the right- and left-hand edges in toward the center by about $^3/_4$ in. (2 cm) and press, then turn the top edge over again by about $1^1/_2$ in. (4 cm) and pin.

2 Load your sewing machine with cotton thread to match the fabric and stitch along the bottom edge of the top fold. By doing this, you are creating the channel at the top of the sack that your drawstring will be passed through. Repeat steps 1 and 2 for the bottom edge.

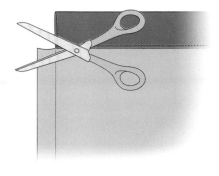

3 Snip into your fabric just underneath the right- and left-hand edges of both channels to release the side edges of the fabric ready for hemming.

4 With right sides together, fold the fabric in half lengthwise, so that the two channels align at the top. Pin along each long side.

5 Once pinned, turn the sack right side out so that you can see your finished stitching and check that it is right in the center. If you are not happy with the position, then keep re-pinning the seams until it's just right. If you are finding this a little tricky, try gently pressing the sack when it is right side out where you would like the seam to be, so that the crease can give you a guideline for pinning. When you are completely happy, turn the sack inside out again and machine stitch each side from bottom to top.

6 Turn the bag right side out. Overstitch around the channels to neaten up any raw edges and firmly link the bottom of the two channels together.

YOU WILL NEED

Fabric cut to the size stated in the pattern

Tape measure

Pins

Sewing machine

Cotton thread

Small, sharp scissors

Fabric scissors

Ribbon cut to the length stated in the pattern

Safety pin

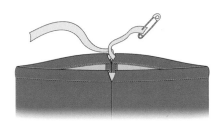

7 Attach a large safety pin to the end of your drawstring or ribbon and thread it through the channels at the top. You can either cut the ribbon into two equal lengths, thread one through each channel, then tie two bows, one at either side, or thread the whole length through both channels and finish with just one bow on the side.

FOR YOUNG ONES

Making stuff for little ones is a great excuse to get really creative in cross stitch. From baby-grows and glow-in-the-dark T-shirts to phone cases inspired by 1950s comics, there are projects here to delight everyone, from the smallest to the biggest kid in your life.

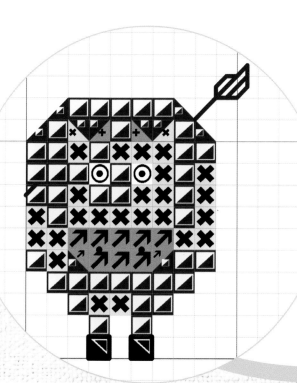

xxxxxxxxxxxxxxxxxxxxxxxxxxxxxxxxxxxx

OUT iN THE BARNYARD

I love these little animals—they make an adorable flock for a nursery. The sheep all follow exactly the same pattern, but as soon as you put French knots into the eyes, they all seem to develop their own unique personalities.

The fluffy sheep are a result of a mistake that I was trying to unpick on another project. The cut and half pulled-out floss (thread) had the consistency of soft sheep's wool. So, if you can bear it, snip away at your perfect stitches and give your work some super texture (and know that mistakes aren't always a bad thing).

PATTERN SKILL LEVEL
✕ ✕ ✕ ✕ ✕

MATERIAL SKILL LEVEL
✕ ✕ ✕ ✕ ✕

YOU WILL NEED

Chart on page 28

10-in. (25-cm) square of 28-count DMC linen, color 3782

DMC stranded cotton embroidery floss (thread) in the following colors: B5200 (white), ECRU (cream), 310 (black), 434 (light brown), 898 (dark brown), 3820 (yellow), 740 (orange), 666 (red), 3354 (pink), 943 (green)

Tapestry needle, size 26

Picture frame with 5-in. (12.5-cm) square internal aperture

Acid-free foam board or a piece of stiff cardboard

Strong thread (pearl cotton is ideal)

Basic kit (see page 8)

FINISHED DESIGN SIZE
4⅜ x 4⅜ in. (11 x 11 cm); 52 x 51 stitches

1 Fold the linen in half across the length and width, and crease it. The point where the creases cross is the center of your fabric.

2 Find the center of the pattern, as indicated by the lines on the chart on page 28. Working from the center outward and following the chart, stitch the barnyard scene (see pages 12–13).

3 Use a small, sharp pair of scissors to very carefully cut some of the top half stitches of the sheep's fleece. Run your finger over the stitches to fluff up the ends of the floss.

4 Mount the embroidery in a picture frame (see page 20). I left the glass out of the picture frame so that little fingers can give the fluffy sheep a stroke.

xxxxxxxxxxxxxxxxxxxxxxxxxxxxxxxxxxxxxxxxxxxx

TOP TIP
Try replacing DMC ECRU with DMC 934 (a brown/black color) to create your very own black sheep.

Thread color key

Symbol	DMC No	Description	Number of strands for cross stitch	Number of strands for backstitch
⬭	B5200	White	2	—
✖	ECRU	Cream	2	—
◩	310	Black	2	1
⬭	434	Light brown	2	—
◪	898	Dark brown	2	1
➕	3820	Yellow	2	1
◀	740	Orange	2	1
✷	666	Red	2	1
➚	3354	Pink	2	—
▤	943	Green	2	1

⊡ This symbol indicates a French knot (see page 14) in black.

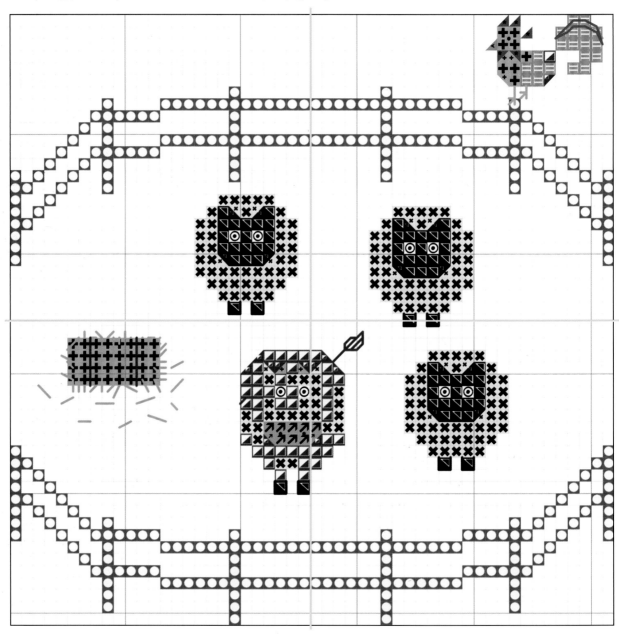

PEEPiNG TED

Sweet ted would make a lovely new baby or christening gift.
It's a keepsake that will look brilliant in a nursery for years.
As the design is in gender-neutral colors, you can begin to
stitch even if you are still in delicious anticipation of whether
the baby is a boy or girl. Just add the given name and date of
birth in your chosen color once you know.

XXXXXXXXXXXXXXXXXXXXXXXXXXX

PATTERN SKILL LEVEL
✗ ✗ ✗ ✗ ✗

MATERIAL SKILL LEVEL
✗ ✗ ✗ ✗ ✗

YOU WILL NEED
Charts on pages 31 and 126–127

10 x 9-in. (25.5 x 23-cm) piece
of 14-count DMC linen aida
(color 842L, Ecru)

DMC stranded cotton embroidery
floss (thread) in the following colors:
3860 (dark brown), 452 (light brown),
310 (black), B5200 (white),
3838 (blue), 725 (yellow), 943 (green),
741 (orange), 208 (purple)

Tapestry needle, size 24

Frame with an aperture of at least
7 x 5 in. (18 x 12.5 cm)

Basic kit (see page 8)

FINISHED DESIGN SIZE
This will depend on the length of the
name you are including, but the
example shown here measures
5³⁄₄ x 4¹⁄₂ in. (14.5 x 11.5 cm);
79 x 64 stitches

XXXXXXXXXXXXXXXXXXXXXXXXX

TOP TIP
Materials and instructions for
framing your finished ted can
be found on page 20. Just
remember that rather than
centering your piece, the edge
of the ted should meet the
bottom and right-hand edges
of the frame.

1 Fold the fabric in half across the length and width, and crease it. The point where the creases cross is the center of your fabric.

2 Find the center of the pattern, as indicated by the lines on the chart opposite. Working from the center outward and following the chart, stitch the teddy bear design (see pages 12–13), completing all the cross stitches before moving on to backstitch.

3 Use small backstitches (see page 14) across single squares to make the lines in teddy's ear.

4 Make sure that the end of your name will not finish further right than the right-hand edge of the teddy. Create your name by choosing the relevant letters from our alphabet patterns on pages 126–127. You will need to leave a space of two squares between each letter. Count the number of squares in the width of each of your letters, then add 2 to each and add them together.

So, using Max as the example:

Capital "M" is 11 squares wide; 11 + 2 = 13
Lower-case "a" is 6 squares wide; 6 + 2 = 8
Lower-case "x" is 8 squares wide; 8 + 2 = 10
13 + 8 + 10 = 31 squares

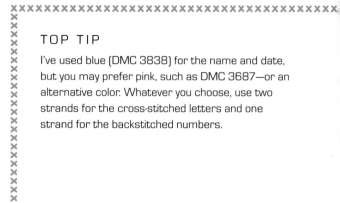

TOP TIP

I've used blue (DMC 3838) for the name and date, but you may prefer pink, such as DMC 3687—or an alternative color. Whatever you choose, use two strands for the cross-stitched letters and one strand for the backstitched numbers.

5 If your name measures less than 79 squares, line up the left-hand and bottom edge of your first letter with the "M" for Max in the pattern.

If your name is more than 79 squares, simply place your first capital letter further to the left. (For example, if your name is 89 squares wide, then move the starting point left by 10 squares.)

6 Format your date by lining up your first number with the first number in the pattern, or with the left-hand edge of your name, whichever is further left. Leave one square between each of your numbers. Stitch the numbers using either long stitch (see page 14) or backstitch.

Thread color key

Symbol	DMC No	Description	Number of strands for cross stitch	Number of strands for backstitch
	3860	Dark brown	2	—
	452	Light brown	2	—
	310	Black	2	—
	B5200	White	2	—
	3838	Blue	2	1
	725	Yellow	—	1
	943	Green	—	1
	741	Orange	—	1
	208	Purple	—	1

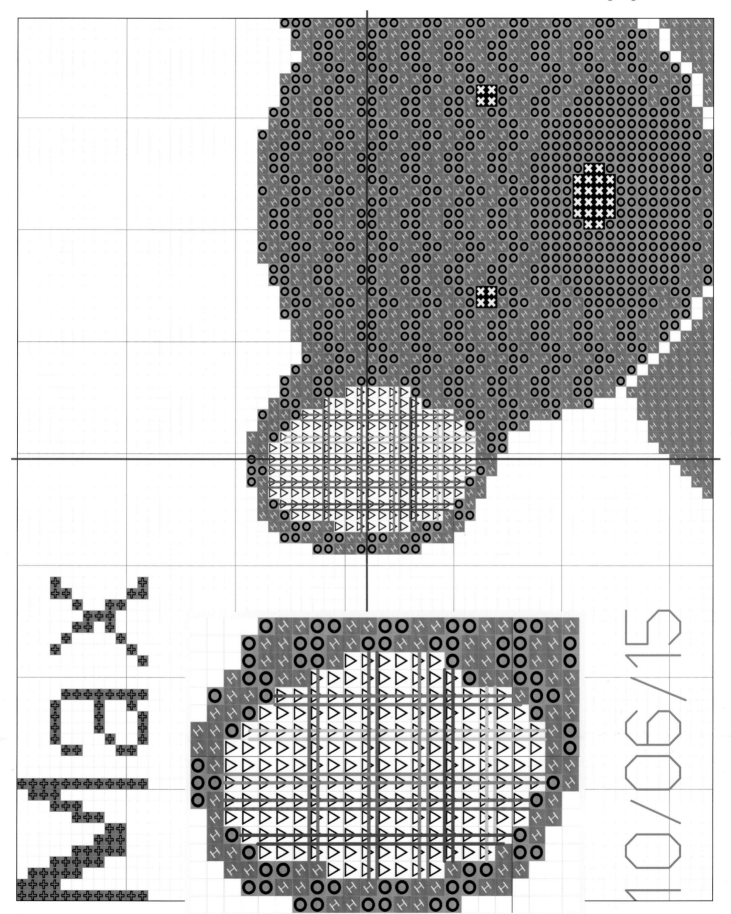

Detail showing backstitch pattern on ear

BUNNIES FOR BABIES

Quick and fun to stitch, these gorgeous little bunnies can adorn only the best-dressed little ones.

1 Prepare your fabric and position your soluble canvas on the garment, following the instructions on page 16.

2 Cross stitch the pattern onto the garment as you would with normal aida, using the grid in the canvas.

3 Again following the instructions on page 17, rinse away the soluble canvas and finish with a second piece of interfacing.

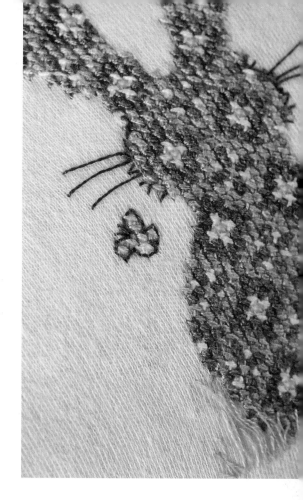

TOP TIP

Once you've finished stitching the long white stitches for the bunny's tail, take small lengths of thread, push your needle underneath the stitches on top of the fabric and tie a small knot in the center of the tail. Snip the thread so that the ends are about ¼ in. (5 mm) long either side of the knot; do this two or three times to create a fluffy, 3-D effect.

PATTERN SKILL LEVEL

✕✕✕✕✕

MATERIAL SKILL LEVEL

✕✕✕✕✕

YOU WILL NEED

Chart on page 35

1 white baby-grow, vest, or T-shirt in the appropriate size

One 4 x 6 in. (10 x 15-cm) piece of DMC soluble canvas

Two 4 x 6-in. (10 x 15-cm) pieces of iron-on interfacing in a weight to match your fabric

DMC stranded cotton embroidery floss (thread) in the following colors:

For blue bunny:
3838 (dark blue), 922 (peach), ECRU (cream), 3840 (light blue), 725 (yellow), 943 (bright green), 317 (dark gray)

For pink bunny:
3840 (light blue), 211 (light purple), B5200 (white), 3354 (pink),

966 (light green), 744 (light yellow), 317 (dark gray)

Embroidery needle, size 4

Cotton thread

Basic kit (see page 8)

FINISHED DESIGN SIZE

2¾ x 4 in. (7 x 10 cm), 36 x 55 stitches

Thread color key

Symbol	Blue bunny DMC No	Blue bunny Description	Pink bunny DMC No	Pink bunny Description	Number of strands for cross stitch	Number of strands for backstitch
▣	3838	Dark blue	3840	Light blue	2	—
✖	922	Peach	211	Light purple	2	—
▲	ECRU	Cream	B5200	White	2	—
◎	3840	Light blue	3354	Pink	2	—
♥	725	Yellow	966	Light green	2	—
●	725	Yellow	744	Light yellow	2	—
▤	943	Bright green	966	Light green	—	1
▤	317	Dark gray	317	Dark gray	—	1
▢	ECRU	Cream	B5200	White	—	1

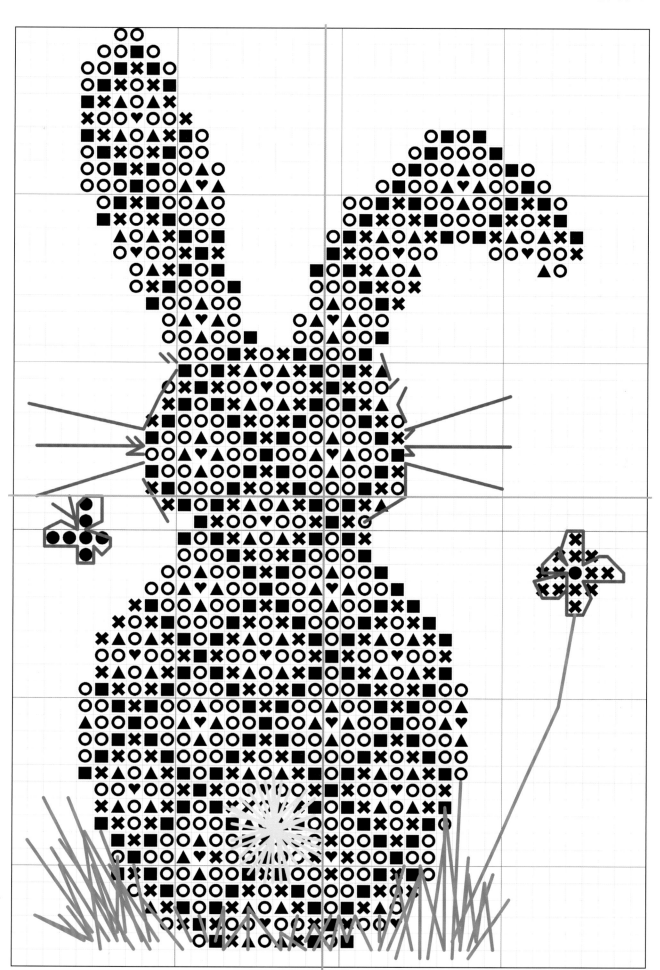

NURSERY BASICS

This bright, chunky pattern is a fun way to help little one learn their ABC and 123. Stitched in bold colors, this design really celebrates the aesthetic of cross stitch. But if you are not so keen on the simple look, this is a project that is perfect to customize. Draw or paint embellishments onto the canvas before you stitch to make it a really special gift.

1 Photocopy each of the patterns in this book at actual size and cut out.

2 Place the pattern over your canvas so that it is perfectly centered and straight. Tape it in place.

3 Use a sharp pin to gently push a small hole through each of the yellow dots of the pattern. Do each dot on the pattern before moving on to step 4.

4 Remove the paper pattern from your canvas. Use the grid you have made to stitch in the normal way, following your pattern. You can break the golden rule of cross stitch for this fabric...you CAN use a knot to secure your thread at the beginning and the end to hold it securely in place.

xxxxxxxxxxxxxxxxxxxxxxxxxxxxxxx

PATTERN SKILL LEVEL
x x x x x

MATERIAL SKILL LEVEL
x x x x x

YOU WILL NEED

Charts on pages 37 and 39

Two 14 x 10-in. (35 x 25-cm) pieces of stretched painting canvas, 100% linen

Anchor Freccia 3-ply crochet thread in the following colors: 00290 (yellow), 00255 (green), 00089 (magenta), 00314 (orange), 00142 (blue), 00046 (red)

Sticky tape

Sharp pin

Tapestry needle, size 22

Basic kit (see page 8)

FINISHED DESIGN SIZE
9½ x 6 in. (24 x 15 cm);
ABC: 27 x 17 stitches; 123: 26 x 17 stitches

Thread color key for ABC

Symbol	Anchor Freccia No	Description	Number of strands for cross stitch	Number of strands for backstitch
⊘	00290	Yellow	1	—
⊞	00255	Green	1	—
●	00089	Pink	1	–
✖	00142	Blue	1	1

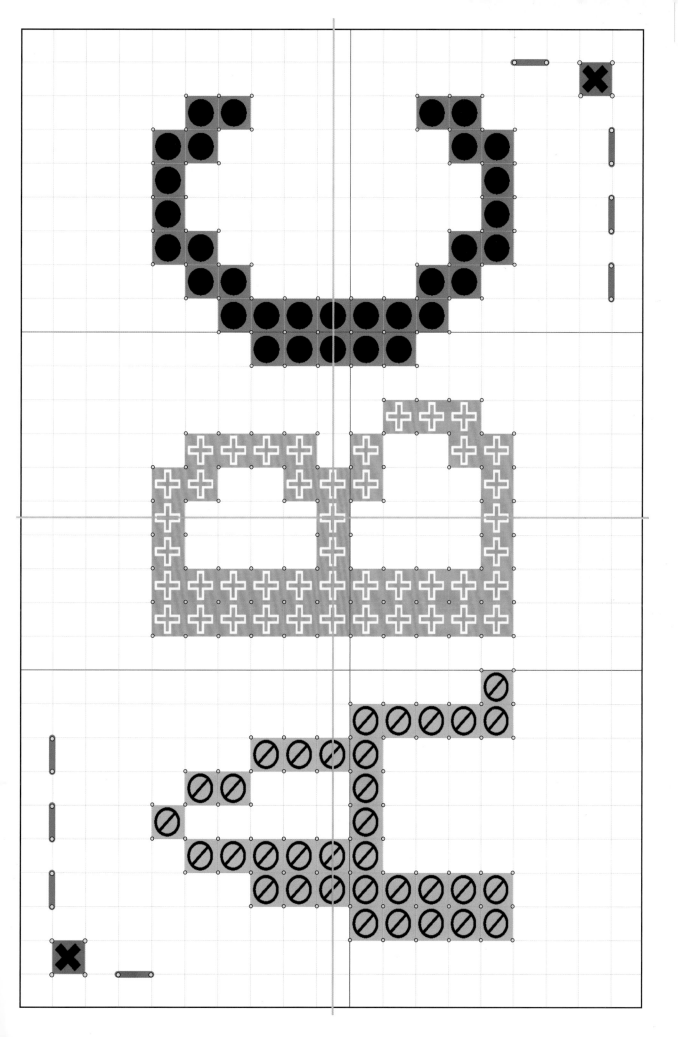

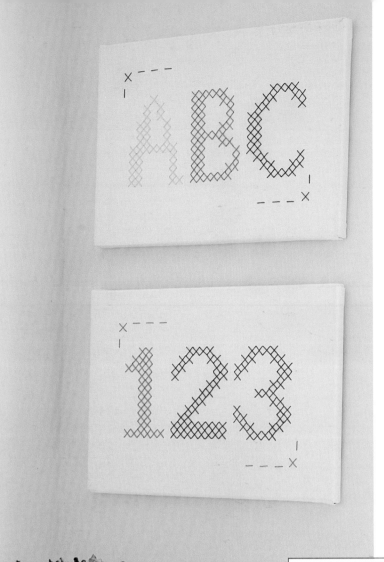

You might find it tricky at first to find where the hole is when bringing your needle up from underneath the canvas. Use the tip of the needle to press gently on the back of the canvas so that you can see where it is, then move it around gently until you find the hole.

5 If you notice your thread becoming at all fluffy, fasten it off and restart with a fresh piece to keep your crosses as neat and striking as possible.

6 No finishing is necessary here. The instant you have finished stitching, you can hang it on the wall. Perfect!

Thread color key for 123

Symbol	Anchor Freccia No	Description	Number of strands for cross stitch	Number of strands for backstitch
⊙	00314	Orange	1	—
✖	00142	Blue	1	—
★	00046	Red	1	—
✛	00255	Green	1	1

TOP TIPS

• The crochet thread used here is quite a lot thicker and tougher than normal cross-stitch floss (thread), so it can be dragged through the canvas without fraying, but this can make it quite hard to thread it through the eye of your needle. Try using a wire needle threader if you are struggling.

• Wrap a piece of scrap material around the edge of your canvas where you are holding it to stop it from getting dirty.

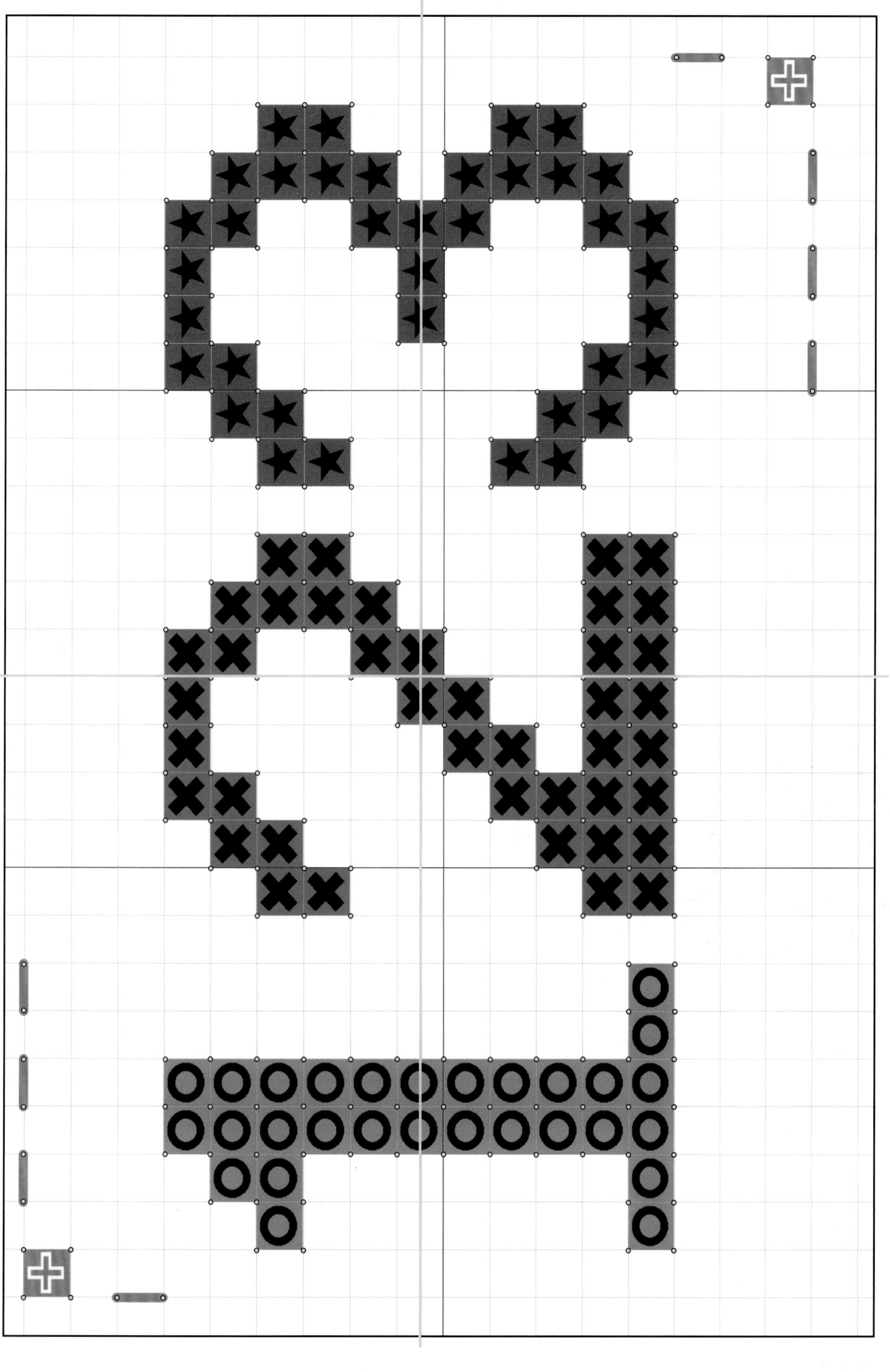

×××××××××××××××××××××××

PATTERN SKILL LEVEL

✕ ✕ ✕ ✕ ✕

MATERIAL SKILL LEVEL

✕ ✕ ✕ ✕ ✕

YOU WILL NEED

Chart on page 41

18-in. (45-cm) square of white 14-count aida cut into nine 6-in. (15-cm) squares

Nine 4-in. (10-cm) squares of backing fabric of your choice

DMC stranded cotton embroidery floss (thread) in the following colors: 3838 (blue), 911 (green), 725 (yellow), 602 (pink), 553 (purple)

Tapestry needle, size 24

Nine 3-in. (7.5-cm) wooden embroidery hoops

Acrylic paints in blue, green, yellow, pink, and purple

Paintbrush

Basic kit (see page 8)

FINISHED DESIGN SIZE

2 x 2 in. (5 x 5 cm); O: 26 x 26 stitches; X: 25 x 26 stitches

TiC-TAC-TOE

Here's a modern twist on a classic game. Simple cross stitches in just one color make these hoops a great project for a beginner. Enjoy!

1 Fold each piece of aida in half across the length and width, and crease it. The point where the creases cross is the center of your fabric.

2 Taking the center of your fabric and chart as your starting point, begin stitching (see pages 12–13). Stitch four pairs of noughts and crosses, using a different color for each pair, then stitch an extra cross in a new color.

3 Paint the embroidery hoops in colors to match the stitching, then frame each nought and cross in a matching hoop (see page 18 for full instructions). Now you're all set to play tic-tac-toe!

Thread color key

Symbol	DMC No	Description	Number of strands for cross stitch
	3838	Blue	2
	911	Green	2
☒	725	Yellow	2
	602	Pink	2
	553	Purple	2

TOP TIP

Tap nine small picture hooks onto the wall in a grid shape so that you can either play the game or simply create some bright wall art.

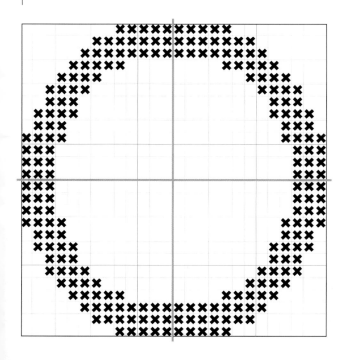

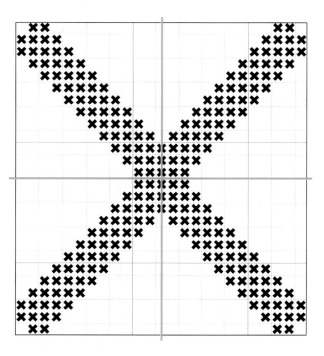

KAPOW! PHONE CASE

Kapow! Take that! Here's a project for loud and proud cross-stitch addicts. These phone covers are made from flexible plastic with pre-punched holes. You can buy them to fit your own phone type (there is a really large selection of sizes and the manufacturers keep up with phone releases really well) and they just slip on as any other phone cover would. Simply stitch into them in the same way you would linen or aida.

xxxxxxxxxxxxxxxxxxxxx

PATTERN SKILL LEVEL

✗ ✗ ✗ ✗ ✗

MATERIAL SKILL LEVEL

✗ ✗ ✗ ✗ ✗

YOU WILL NEED

Chart on page 43

Stitchable phone case cover (easy to find on the internet in sizes to suit all phone types)

DMC stranded cotton embroidery floss (thread) in the following colors: B5200 (white), 995 (blue), 725 (yellow), 817 (red), 317 (gray)

Tapestry needle, size 26

Basic kit (see page 8)

FINISHED DESIGN SIZE

4¾ x 2¼ in. (12 x 5.5 cm); 89 x 36 stitches

1 Find the center of the pattern, as indicated by the lines on the chart on page 43. Rather than measure, count the number of holes across and down on your phone cover to ensure that you start exactly in the middle, as there is no room for error. If your cover is slightly smaller than this pattern, simply take off one or two rows and/or columns from the outside of this pattern. Similarly, if your cover is larger, either stitch a one-color border until you reach the edge or

continue the spikes of the bubble outward. The hole for your camera may also be larger or smaller, so adapt as necessary.

2 Working from the center outward and following the chart, stitch the motif (see pages 12–13).

3 When you have finished your stitching, simply slip the cover onto your phone. No further making up required—hurrah!

xxxxxxxxxxxxxxxxxxxxxxx

TOP TIP

I stitched a cover for an iPhone 5s. If your phone cover is bit larger than this, just continue the pattern out to the edge.

Thread color key

Symbol	DMC No	Description	Number of strands for cross stitch
◪	B5200	White	1
◆	995	Blue	1
◉	725	Yellow	1
✖	817	Red	1
▬	317	Gray	1

GLOW-iN-THE-DARK SKULL PATCHES

This project combines two of my favorite cross-stitch supplies—soluble canvas and glow-in-the-dark thread. Stitch these fun little skulls onto a piece of clothing of your choice (high-quality cotton T-shirts, thin denim, and jersey fabric all work really well). My son kept dragging me off to hide in the cupboard so we could see his T-shirt glow in the dark!

PATTERN SKILL LEVEL
✗ ✗ ✗ ✗ ✗

MATERIAL SKILL LEVEL
✗ ✗ ✗ ✗ ✗

YOU WILL NEED
Chart on page 46

Garment of your choice

6-in. (15-cm) square of DMC soluble canvas

Two 8-in. (20-cm) squares of iron-on interfacing in a weight to match your clothing

DMC stranded cotton embroidery floss (thread) in the following colors:

For the pink skull:
3865 (white), E940 (glow-in-the-dark), 317 (dark gray), 602 (dark pink), 604 (light pink)

For the gray skull:
B5200 (white), E940 (glow-in-the-dark), 317 (dark gray), 414 (mid gray), 415 (light gray), 817 (red)

Embroidery needle, size 4

7-in. (18-cm) embroidery hoop

FINISHED DESIGN SIZE
3½ x 3½ in. (9 x 9 cm);
51 x 49 stitches

1 Prepare your fabric and position your soluble canvas, following the instructions on page 16.

2 Cross stitch the pattern onto your fabric as you would with normal aida, using the grid in the canvas.

3 Again following the instructions on page 17, rinse away the canvas and finish with a second piece of interfacing.

TOP TIP
Glow-in-the-dark thread is "solar powered," so if the light fades gradually it may not shine with all its might. Hold your piece under a bright light for a few seconds and it will glow away again happily.

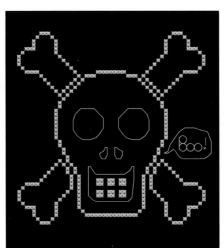

This chart shows which parts of the gray skull design glow in the dark. (See note on page 46.)

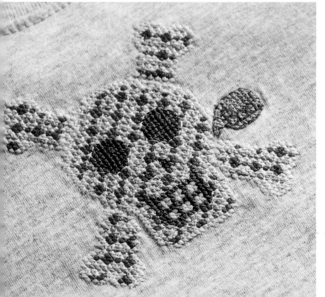

TANGLE ALERT

Stitch your glow-in-the-dark thread first, so that you don't get in a muddle with the regular white thread.

Thread color key for the skulls

Symbol	Gray skull		Pink skull		Number of strands for cross stitch	Number of strands for long stitch
	DMC No	Description	DMC No	Description		
◉	3865	White	3865	White	2	—
☾	E940	Glow-in-the-dark	E940	Glow-in-the-dark	2	1 (see note)
✖	317	Dark gray	317	Dark gray	2	1
■	414	Mid gray	602	Dark pink	2	—
◪	415	Light gray	604	Light pink	2	—
⬦	817	Red	604	Light pink	2	—

Note: On the pink version, I stitched the speech bubble and "Boo!" in dark gray, instead of glow-in-the-dark, so that it would show up better during the day.

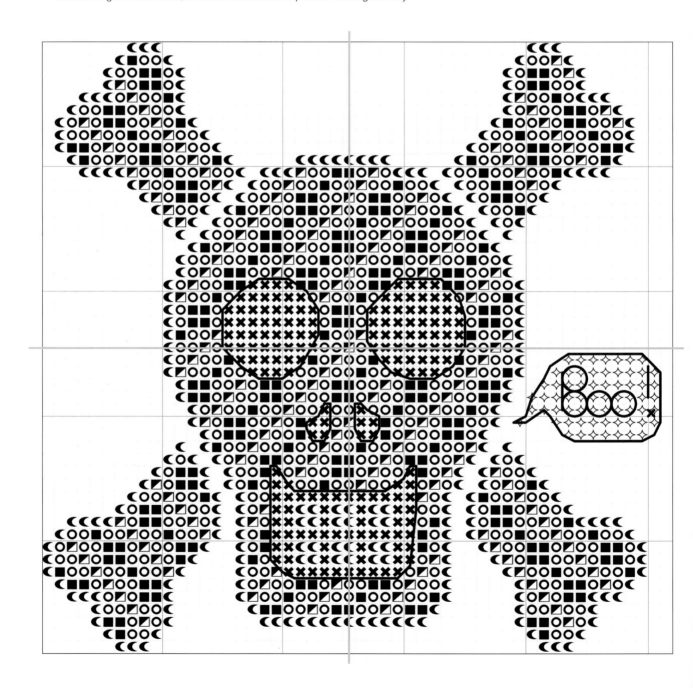

SPRING BUNTING

I do love a bit of bunting, so cross-stitched bunting is really up my street. This is such a pretty but sophisticated decoration, perfect to adorn the bedroom of an older girl before all the posters of boy bands take over.

1 Fold each piece of aida in half across the length and width and crease. Where the creases cross is the center of your fabric.

2 Stitch each flag onto one piece of your rectangular aida fabric so that you can easily use an embroidery hoop. Taking the center of your fabric and chart as the starting point, begin stitching (see pages 12–13).

3 When you have completed your stitching, wash each piece carefully following the instructions on page 15. Once dry, cut out the triangle, leaving at least ³/₄ in. (2 cm) or eight squares of fabric above the very top stitches, ³/₄ in. (2 cm) around the outer edge of the triangle, and 2¹/₂ in. (6 cm) below the very bottom stitch.

4 Cut your five pieces of backing fabric down to the same size as your flags. Place your first cross-stitch flag right side up on a flat surface. Lay the first backing triangle on top, right side down, so that the edges match. Pin the two pieces together along the two long sides of the triangle.

xxxxxxxxxxxxxxxxxxxxxxxxxxxxxxxxx

PATTERN SKILL LEVEL
x x x x x

MATERIAL SKILL LEVEL
x x x x x

YOU WILL NEED
Charts on pages 48–51

Five 7 x 9-in. (18 x 23-cm) pieces of 14-count DMC linen aida (color 842L Ecru)

Five 7 x 9-in. (18 x 23-cm) pieces of backing fabric of your choice (linen works well)

DMC stranded cotton embroidery floss (thread) in the following colors: B5200 (white), 807 (blue), 3731 (pink), 470 (green), 728 (yellow), 3837 (purple)

2¹/₄ yd (2 m) cream bias binding, 1 in. (25 mm) wide

Tapestry needle, size 24

Blunt knitting needle

Basic kit (page 8)

FINISHED DESIGN SIZE
3³/₄ x 4³/₄ in. (9.5 x 12 cm); 52 x 65 stitches

Finished flag: 4³/₄ in. (12 cm) across the top and 5³/₄ in. (14.5 cm) from the top of the flag to the bottom point of the triangle

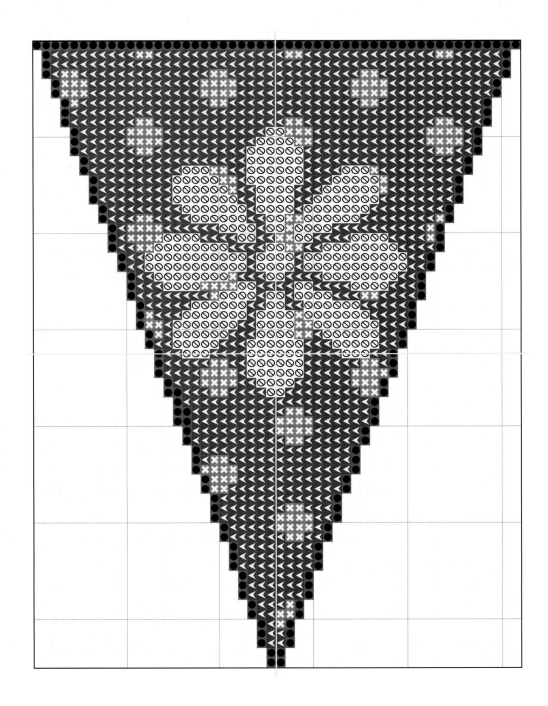

Thread color key

Symbol	DMC No	Description	Number of strands for cross stitch
⊘	B5200	White	2
⊠	470	Green	2
●	3731	Pink	2
◀	3837	Purple	2

5 Turn the flag over so you can now see the reverse of your stitching. Using the edge of the stitches as a guide, machine stitch along the two long edges about $3/8$ in. (1 cm) from the edge of the finished stitching. Leave the short top edge open. Turn the flag right side out and use a blunt knitting needle to push out the point.

6 Repeat steps 4 and 5 for each of your flags.

7 Fold your bias binding in half lengthwise and press to get a good crease. Place your first flag in the center of the binding. Tuck the top short edge of the flag into the fold in the binding and pin the flag in place. Continue pinning the flags to the binding, leaving about 2 in. (5 cm) between each flag.

8 When you are happy with the positioning, stitch along the bottom edge of the binding. This should securely catch all of your flags.

9 Stitch a turn-up hem at either end of the bias binding or leave it unfinished for a more rustic look.

10 Hang the bunting in a prominent place and smile with satisfaction.

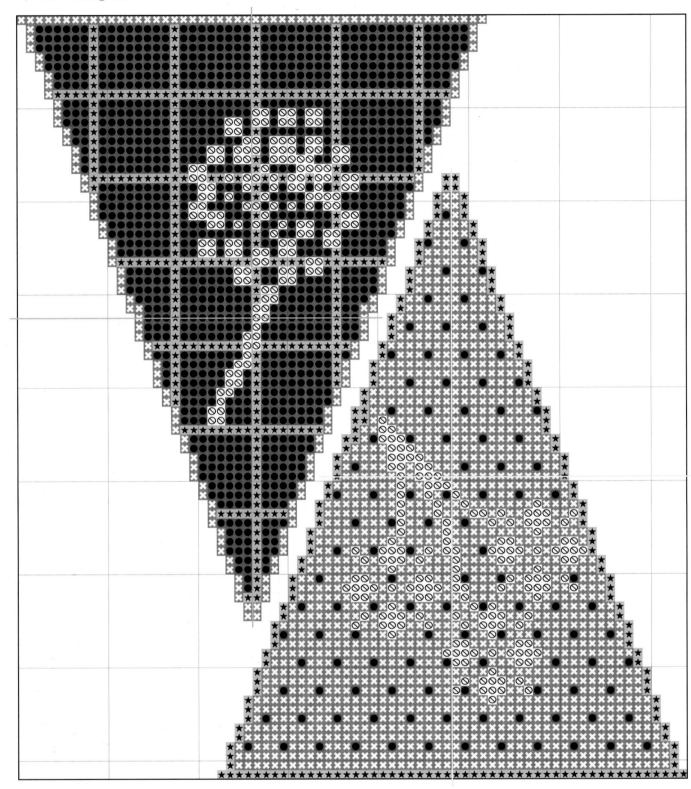

Thread color key

Symbol	DMC No	Description	Number of strands for cross stitch
⊘	B5200	White	2
●	3731	Pink	2
✕	470	Green	2
★	728	Yellow	2

Note: The flags on these charts are placed closely together for illustration purposes only. Each flag should be stitched on its own separate rectangle of aida.

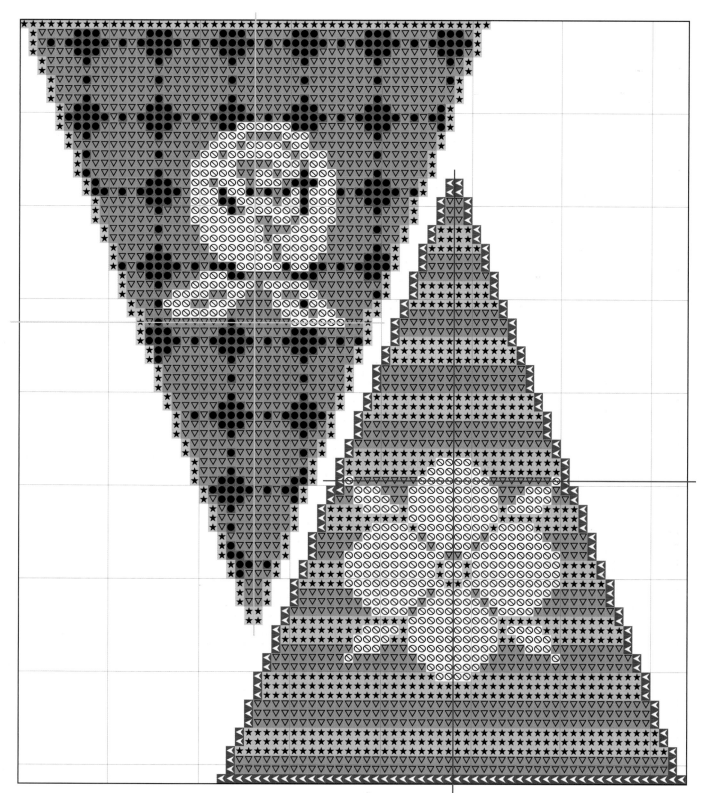

Thread color key

Symbol	DMC No	Description	Number of strands for cross stitch
⊘	B5200	White	2
▽	807	Blue	2
●	3731	Pink	2
★	728	Yellow	2
◀	3837	Purple	2

FOR A
SPECIAL OCCASION

It is a delicious feeling to curl up on the sofa and, stitch by stitch, create something that you know will be treasured. These keepsakes for some big occasions in life will be appreciated, cherished, and admired year after year.

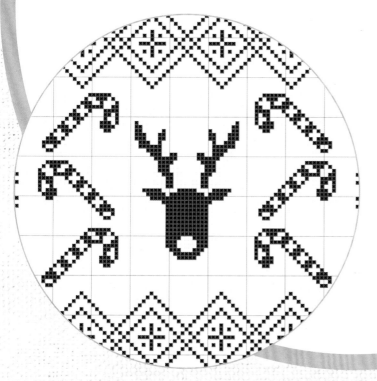

×××××××××××××××××××××××××××

SECRET LOVE NOTE

PATTERN SKILL LEVEL
× × × × ×

MATERIAL SKILL LEVEL
× × × × ×

YOU WILL NEED
Charts on pages 56–57

7 x 9 in. (18 x 23 cm) 28-count
Zweigart Cashel linen in Ice Blue

DMC stranded cotton embroidery
floss (thread) in 603 (bright pink)

Tapestry needle, size 26

Cardstock, approx. 5 x 8 in.
(138 x 200 mm)

White tri-fold aperture greeting
card, approx. 5½ x 8½ in.
(UK A5 size)

Acid-free mounting tape

Basic kit (see page 8)

Double-sided tape

FINISHED DESIGN SIZE
3¼ x 3 in. (8 x 7.5 cm);
45 x 41 stitches

Card size: US A9 (5½ x 8½ in.);
UK A5 (148 x 210 mm)

Send your valentine a secret message that can only be seen when the light shines on the card from a certain angle. I first spotted this super-simple "hidden message" cross-stitch technique, in a piece by Clara Rouhani, on Pinterest (a great source of stitching inspiration). All you need to do is stitch some of your stitches in the wrong direction and they will reflect the light differently. Clever, huh?

1 Fold the fabric in half across the length and width, and crease it. The point where the creases cross is the center of your fabric.

2 Choose your initials from the alphabet pattern provided. For the first initial ("H" in our example), leave a one square gap between the right-hand edge of the letter and the "+." The top stitches of your letter should be three squares up from the top of the "+." The second initial should begin one square to the right of the "+" and one square above the top of the "+."

3 Find the center of the pattern, as indicated by the lines on the chart on page 57. Working from the center outward and following the chart, stitch the opposite-stitching-direction stitches (that is, the "wrong-direction" stitches) first. This means that if you normally work stitches from bottom left to top right, you will instead work from bottom right to top left. Then complete the design as usual (see pages 12–13).

4 Cut a piece of cardstock about ⅜ in. (1 cm) shorter and narrower than your greetings card. Lace up your finished piece following steps 1–6 of the instructions for "How to mount embroidery in a picture frame" on page 20. Once laced, use mounting tape to stick your finished stitching to the card so that the design is centered inside the aperture.

5 Fold down the outside flap of the card to hide the back of your stitches and stick in place with double-sided tape.

6 Write in your card and deliver it to your beloved.

Secret Love Note alphabet chart

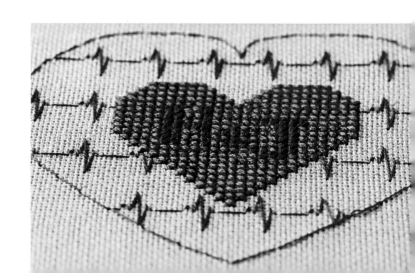

TOP TIP

Stitch all the "wrong-way" stitches first.
If you are an experienced stitcher
entrenched in your usual way of stitching,
this can feeling like trying to write with the
opposite hand to normal!

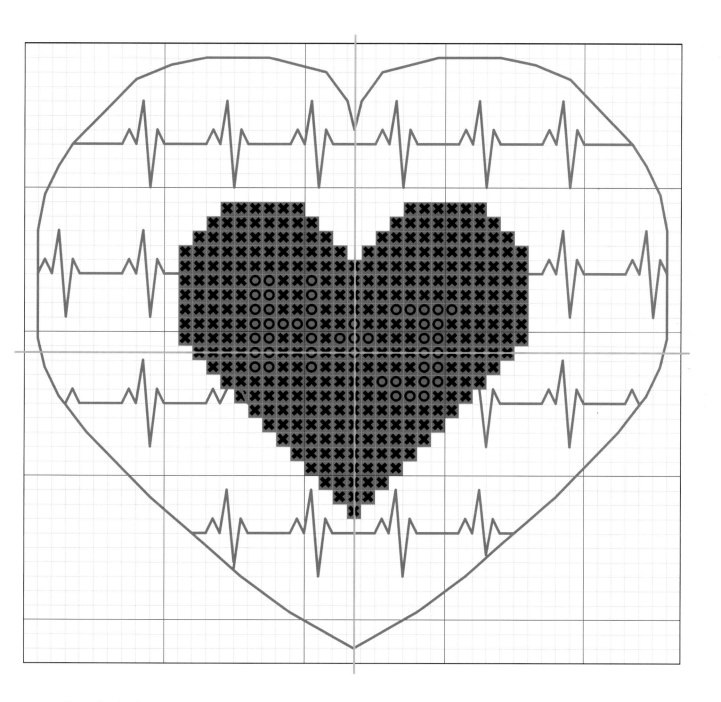

Thread color key

Symbol	DMC No	Description	Number of strands for cross stitch	Number of strands for long stitch
◉	603	Bright pink	2—opposite stitching direction	—
✖	603	Bright pink	2—usual stitching direction	—
▱	603	Bright pink	—	1

xxxxxxxxxxxxxxxxxxxxxxxxxxxx

PATTERN SKILL LEVEL

✗ ✗ ✗ ✗ ✗

MATERIAL SKILL LEVEL

✗ ✗ ✗ ✗ ✗

YOU WILL NEED

Charts on pages 60–61

Two 6-in. (15-cm) squares of
28-count Zweigart Cashel linen in
white for Snowflakes 1 and 2

One 6-in. (15-cm) square of
28-count Zweigart Cashel linen in
pale blue for Snowflake 3

Three 4-in. (10-cm) squares of
backing fabric (I used pale blue felt)

DMC stranded cotton embroidery
floss (thread) in 800 (light blue)

DMC light effects floss (thread) in
the following colors: E334 (metallic
light blue), E316 (metallic light pink),
E415 (metallic light silver),
E317 (metallic dark silver),
E3843 (metallic bright blue)

Three 8-in. (20-cm) lengths
of ribbon

Tapestry needle, size 26

Pearl cotton thread

Three 3-in. (7.5-cm) embroidery
hoops

Silver acrylic paint

Paintbrush

Basic kit (see page 8)

FINISHED DESIGN SIZE

Snowflake 1: 2¼ x 2½ in. (5.75 x
6.25 cm); 29 x 33 stitches

Snowflake 2: 2¼ x 2¼ in. (5.75 x
5.75 cm); 29 x 29 stitches

Snowflake 3: 2½ x 2½ in. (6.25 x
6.25 cm); 31 x 33 stitches

LET iT SNOW!

Every snowflake is unique and these three are no
exception. Mounted in silver embroidery hoops, these
are Christmas tree ornaments that you can enjoy year
after year. And you get to learn a new skill here, with
a little bit of tweeding.

1 So, tweeding... Put simply, this is just threading
your needle with two or more strands of floss
(thread), each a different color, and stitching as
normal. In this case, each snowflake is stitched in one
shade, but that shade is made of up three strands of
floss, each of a different color. Are you still with me?

2 Cut the same length of each of the three flosses
(threads). Keep the length short (around 12 in./
30 cm), as metallic flosses can fray and tangle more
easily than their cotton cousins. Separate one strand
from each length. Combine these three strands into one
and thread your needle.

3 Fold each piece of linen in half across the length
and width, and crease it. The point where the
creases cross is the center of your fabric.

4 Find the center of each pattern, as indicated by the
lines on the charts on pages 60–61. Working from
the center outward and following the charts, stitch
each snowflake motif (see pages 12–13).

5 Paint the outer ring of the embroidery hoops
silver, then leave to dry. Frame your embroideries
in the hoops (see page 18 for full instructions).

Snowflake 1

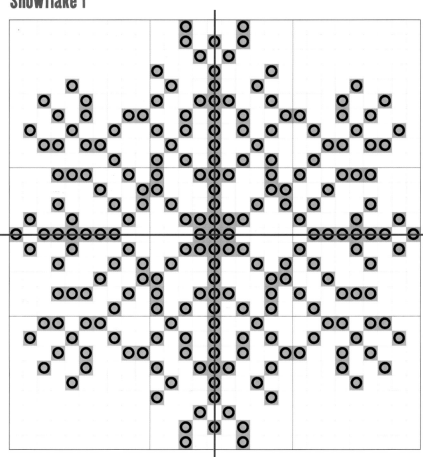

TANGLE ALERT

The flosses may become
more twisted than usual,
so hold your stitching up
so that the needle can
dangle and untangle.

Thread color key

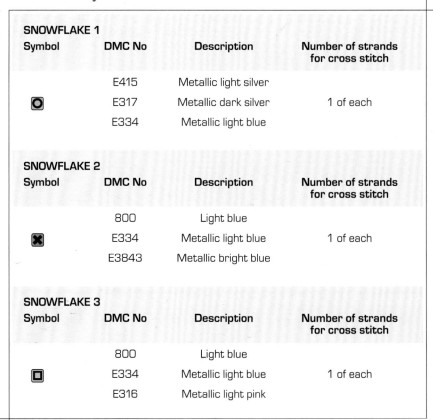

SNOWFLAKE 1

Symbol	DMC No	Description	Number of strands for cross stitch
	E415	Metallic light silver	
⊙	E317	Metallic dark silver	1 of each
	E334	Metallic light blue	

SNOWFLAKE 2

Symbol	DMC No	Description	Number of strands for cross stitch
	800	Light blue	
✖	E334	Metallic light blue	1 of each
	E3843	Metallic bright blue	

SNOWFLAKE 3

Symbol	DMC No	Description	Number of strands for cross stitch
	800	Light blue	
▣	E334	Metallic light blue	1 of each
	E316	Metallic light pink	

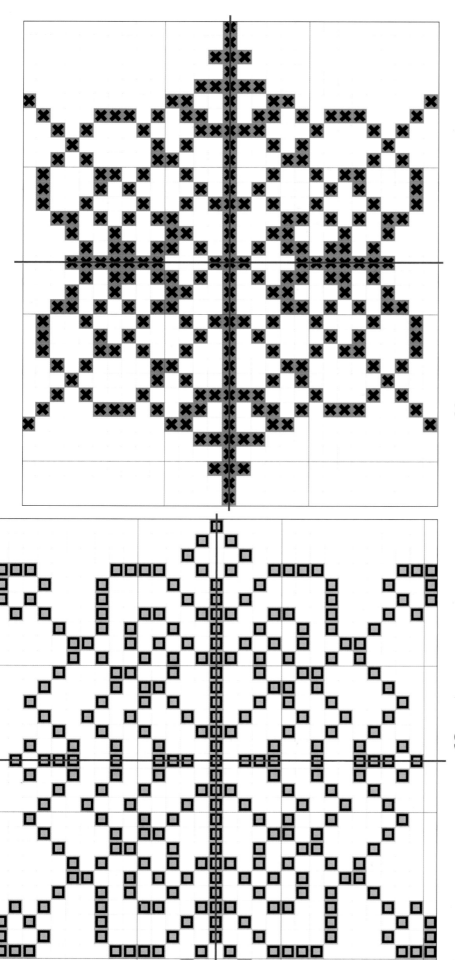

Snowflake 2

Snowflake 3

TAG iT UP

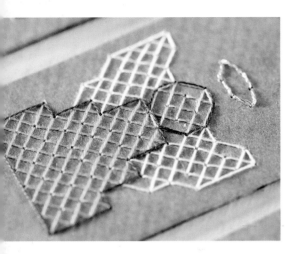

These cute little Christmas gift tags are really easy to make and could be kept as decorations to hang on the tree. You could also use the same patterns to make Christmas cards.

1 Photocopy each of the patterns in this book at actual size and cut out.

2 Place one gift tag on top of your craft mat, cork board, paper pad, or similar. Cover with the pattern so that it is straight and in line with the tag.

3 If you are right-handed, hold the pattern still and in place with your left hand. Use a thumb tack (drawing pin) to gently push a small hole through each of the yellow dots of the pattern, taking care not to crease the card. There's no need to push the tack all the way through the tag—pricking the surface will be fine.

4 You can now use your sharp needle to push all the way through the small holes you have made. Then use the grid you have made to stitch the pattern in the normal way.

5 Once you have finished your stitching, use double-sided tape to firmly stick a blank tag to the reverse to cover the back of your stitches.

6 Write your loved one's name on the tag, then give with pride!

XXXXXXXXXXXXXXXXXXXXXXXXXXXXXXXXXXXXXXXXXXXXXXXXXXXXXXXXXXXXXXXXXXXXXXXXXXXXXXXX

PATTERN SKILL LEVEL
x x x x x

MATERIAL SKILL LEVEL
x x x x x

YOU WILL NEED
Charts on pages 64–65

Ten 1³/₄ x 3¹/₂-in. (4.5 x 9-cm) sturdy brown card gift tags with string

DMC stranded cotton embroidery floss (thread) in the following colors: B5200 (white), 310 (black), 801 (brown), 817 (red), 699 (green), 720 (orange), 597 (light blue), 3326 (light pink), 3607 (bright pink), 725 (yellow)

Kreinik #004 very fine metallic thread in 002J (gold)

Embroidery needle, size 4

Craft mat, cork board, paper pad, or similar

Thumb tack (drawing pin)

Double-sided tape

Basic kit (see page 8)

FINISHED DESIGN SIZE
Tree: 1¹/₈ x 2¹/₁₆ in. (2.9 x 5.2 cm); 7 x 13 stitches

Angel: 1⁷/₁₆ x 1¹⁵/₁₆ in. (3.6 x 4.9 cm); 9 x 12 stitches

Santa: 1⁵/₁₆ x 2¹/₁₆ in. (3.3 x 5.2 cm); 8 x 13 stitches

Snowman: 1¹/₈ x 2¹/₁₆ in. (2.9 x 5.2 cm); 7 x 13 stitches

Robin: 1⁵/₁₆ x 1³/₄ in. (3.3 x 4.5 cm); 8 x 11 stitches

Thread color key

Symbol	DMC No	Description	Number of strands for cross stitch	Number of strands for long stitch
⊠	B5200	White	1	1
◈	310	Black	1	1
◉	801	Brown	1	1
▪	817	Red	1	1
⊞	699	Green	1	—
▽	720	Orange	1	—
▫	597	Light blue	1	—
⊘	3326	Light pink	1	—
●	3607	Bright pink	1	—
◣	725	Yellow	1	1

Symbol	Kreinik #004 very fine	Description	Number of strands for cross stitch	Number of strands for long stitch
⊟	002J	Gold	—	1

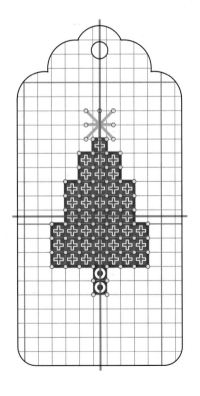

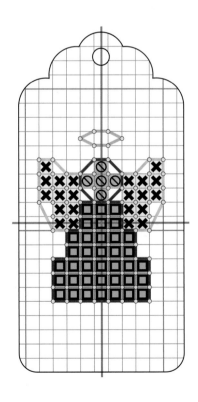

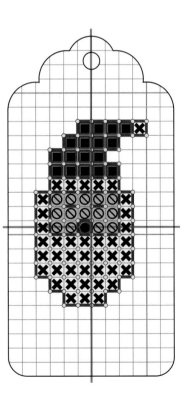

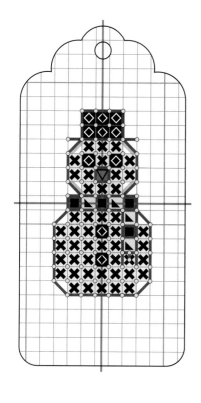

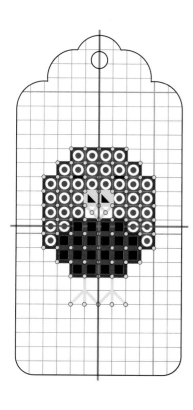

xxxxxxxxxxxxxxxxxxxxxxxxxxxxxxxx

PATTERN SKILL LEVEL
✗ ✗ ✗ ✗ ✗

MATERIAL SKILL LEVEL
✗ ✗ ✗ ✗ ✗

YOU WILL NEED

Charts on pages 68–69

Four 2¾ x 2¾-in. (7 x 7-cm) pieces of DMC soluble canvas

Four white or cream square linen napkins in a size of your choice

DMC stranded cotton embroidery floss (thread) in the following colors: 316 (pink), 807 (blue), 704 (green), 3746 (purple)

DMC light effects floss (thread) in the following colors: E3852 (metallic gold), E3849 (metallic blue), E703 (metallic green), E316 (metallic pink)

Embroidery needle, size 5

Basic kit (see page 8)

FINISHED DESIGN SIZE

Cake: 1½ x 2¼ in. (4 x 5.5 cm); 23 x 31 stitches

Champagne: 1⅜ x 2½ in. (3 x 6.5 cm); 18 x 34 stitches

Gift: 1½ x 1¾ in. (4 x 4.5 cm); 20 x 25 stitches

Balloons: 2 x 2½ in. (5 x 6.5 cm); 27 x 35 stitches

BIRTHDAY NAPKINS

Cake, balloons, gifts, and a glass of bubbles...what more do you need for a great birthday? This set of four napkins will make a birthday treat even more special.

1 Cut your soluble canvas into four pieces measuring exactly 40 x 40 squares, 2¾ x 2¾ in. (7 x 7 cm).

2 Place one piece in the corner of each napkin at a 45-degree angle. Make sure that all four pieces of canvas are in the same place and at the same angle on each napkin. Pin them in place, make sure they look the same, then baste (tack) around the edge.

3 Cross stitch the patterns onto your fabric as you would with normal aida, using the grid in the canvas (see page 16). Note that there is no need to use any iron-on interfacing with this project, as the linen will hold its shape while you stitch.

4 Finish all the cross stitches, then move on to the backstitches. Keep the metallic thread short, as it can fray and tangle easily.

5 Once each napkin is complete, rinse away the soluble canvas (see page 17).

xxxxxxxxxxxxxxxxxxxxxxxxxxxxxxxxxxxxxxxxxxxxxxxxxx

TOP TIP

If the back of your stitches is a little untidy, fear not! Simply iron on a piece of lightweight fusible interfacing to cover it up. No one will ever know!

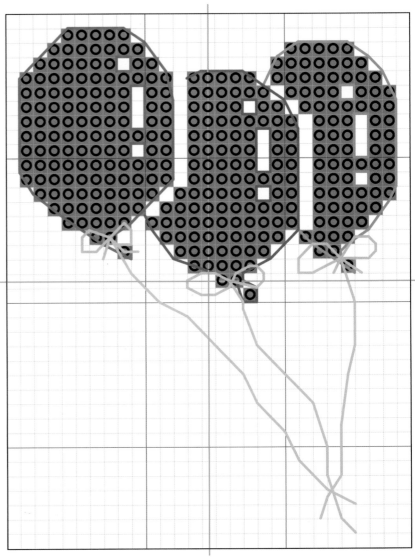

Thread color key

Symbol	DMC No	Description	Number of strands for cross stitch	Number of strands for long stitch
◉	3746	Purple	2	—
▽	316	Pink	2	—
✖	807	Blue	2	—
⊞	704	Green	2	—
⊟	E3852	Metallic gold	—	1
⊟	E316	Metallic pink	—	1
⊟	E3849	Metallic blue	—	1
⊟	E703	Metallic green	—	1

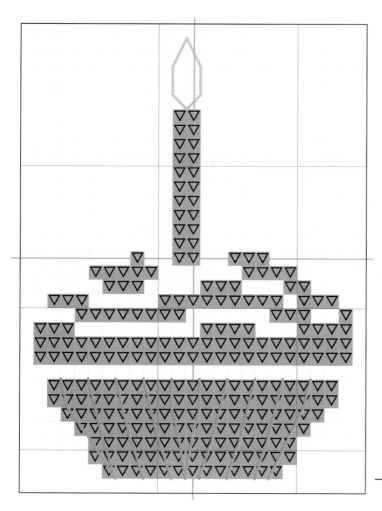

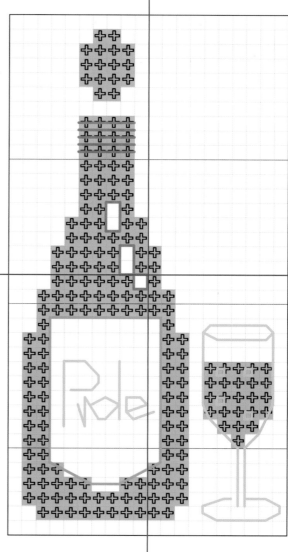

CHRiSTMAS SACK

PATTERN SKILL LEVEL
✕ ✕ ✕ ✕ ✕

MATERIAL SKILL LEVEL
✕ ✕ ✕ ✕ ✕

YOU WILL NEED

Charts on pages 72 and 74–75

26 x 14 in. (65 x 35 cm) DMC 28-count linen in color 3865

DMC stranded cotton embroidery floss (thread) in 347 (red)

26 x 59 in. (65 x150 cm) red linen

Tapestry needle, size 26

Cream and red cotton sewing threads

2¼ yd (2 m) cream velvet ribbon, 1½ in. (36 mm) wide

Large safety pin

Basic kit (see page 8)

FINISHED DESIGN SIZE

20½ x 8½ in. (52 x 21.5 cm); 280 x 118 stitches

Finished sack size: 20 x 27½ in. (50 x 70 cm)

Ah... the excitement of Christmas Eve as a child! Do you remember hanging your Christmas stocking, pillowcase, or sack at the end of your bed? Waking up to find that Santa had been? Just magic! This will surely become a treasured family heirloom.

1 Fold the cream linen in half across the length and width, and crease it. The point where the creases cross is the center of your fabric.

2 Find the center of the pattern, as indicated by the lines on the charts on pages 74–75. Working from the center outward and following the chart, begin stitching (see pages 12–13).

3 Make up your name from the alphabet provided. Leaving two stitches between each letter, work out where the center of your name will be, then align it with the center of the pattern. The top stitch of your letters should begin after a three-square gap from the bottom of the lower diamond banner.

The pattern is divided into two parts, plus the alphabet chart on page 72.

Left side (page 74)   Right side (page 75)

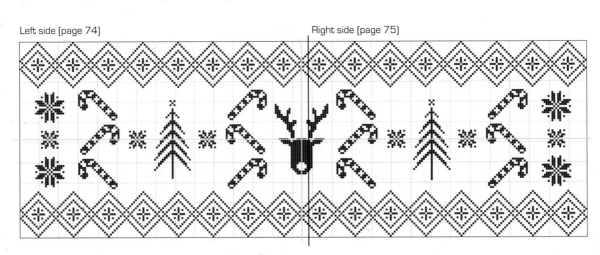

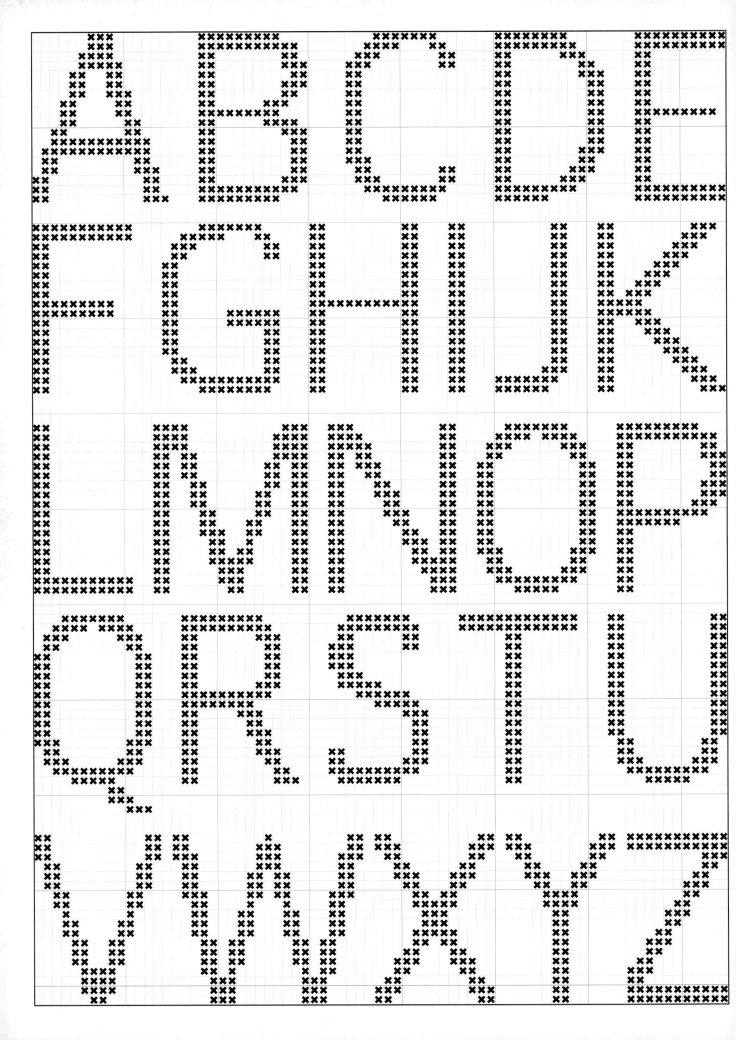

4 Wash and press your finished cross-stitched piece, following the instructions on page 15. Fold the top and bottom edges under, leaving about a 5-square width beyond the bottom and top edges of the stitches. Using an iron, carefully press into a sharp crease, then cut away the excess fabric, about $^3/_8$ in. (1 cm) from the crease.

5 Fold your piece of red linen in half, right side out. Pin your finished stitching in place, with the top edge about 12 in. (30 cm) from the top of the linen, taking care to keep it straight.

6 Using backstitch (see page 14) and cream cotton sewing thread, hand stitch your piece to the red linen along the top and bottom edges, about $^1/_8$ in. (3 mm) from the edge. Use the holes in the linen to stitch in a nice straight line.

7 Make up the drawstring sack, following the instructions on page 23. When checking that the pattern is centered before sewing up, make sure that the right- and left-hand edges are caught evenly in the seams so that the pattern finishes at the same point on each side (the very last few stitches should be hidden in the seam).

8 Hang the sack on the end of your bed on Christmas Eve and keep your fingers crossed that you are on Santa's "nice" list.

Thread color key

Symbol	DMC No	Description	Number of strands for cross stitch
✖	347	Red	2

TOP TIP

Count carefully here. Each little icon on the chart is separate, so it would be easy to miscount by one square which will throw the symmetry of the pattern off entirely... so, no pressure! Count carefully from the nearest completed stitch, then cross reference with the top and bottom banner and anything else you can, to make sure that you are stitching in exactly the right place to avoid a lot of unpicking.

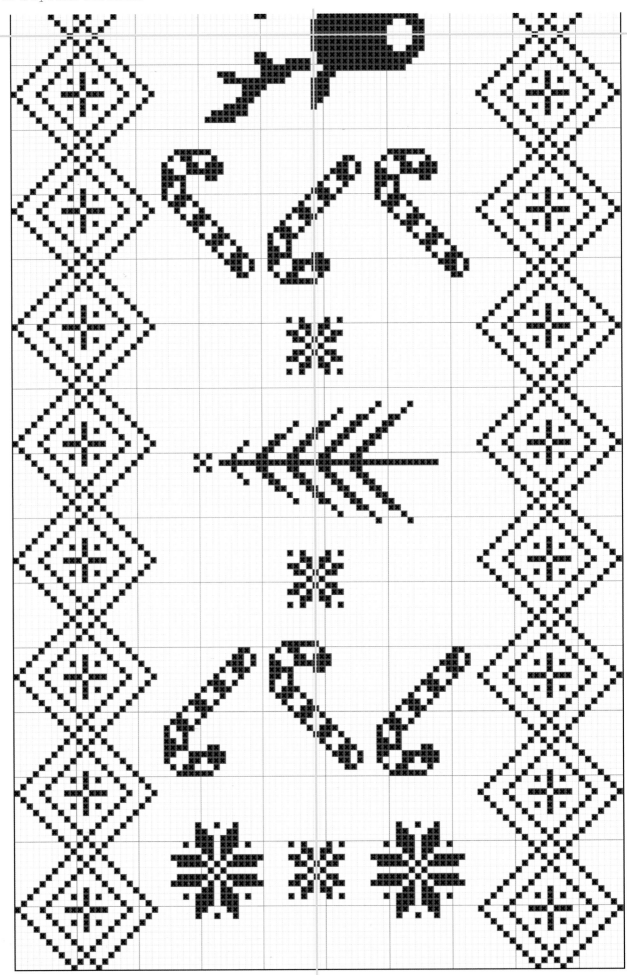

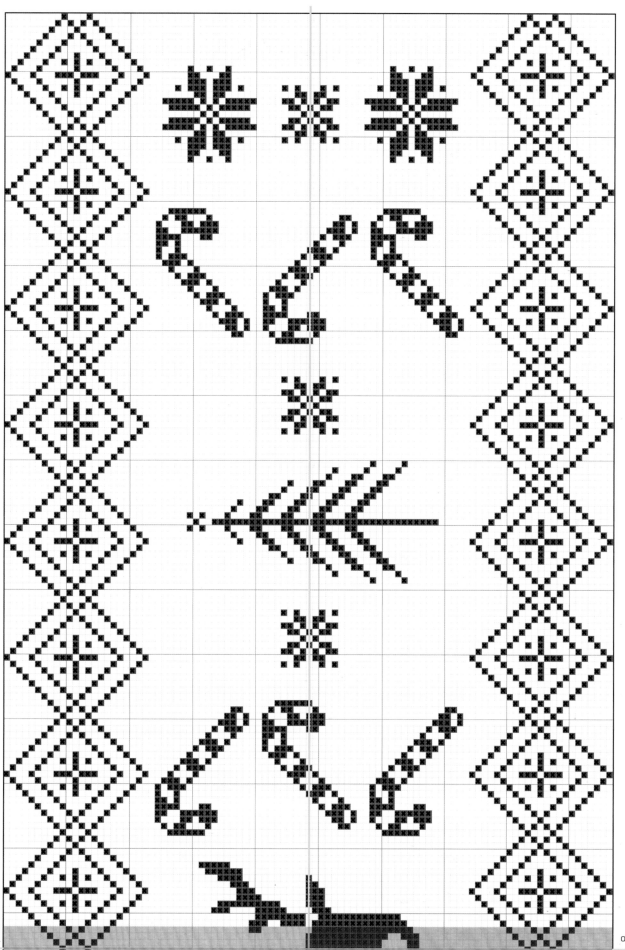

overlap

CHAPTER 3

FOR A NATURE LOVER

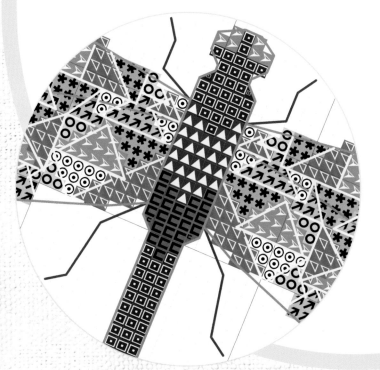

If Mother Nature was indeed a person, would she stitch? Probably. She has certainly provided us with a wealth of beautiful shapes, patterns, and colors. So let's celebrate it, with an array of flora- and fauna-inspired patterns designed to bring a little of the outside in.

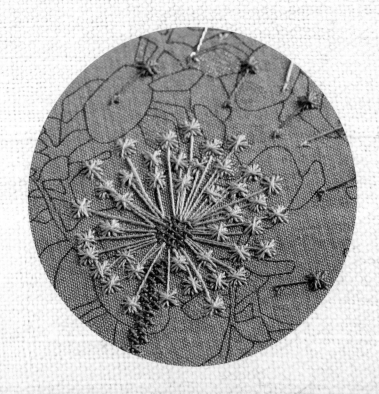

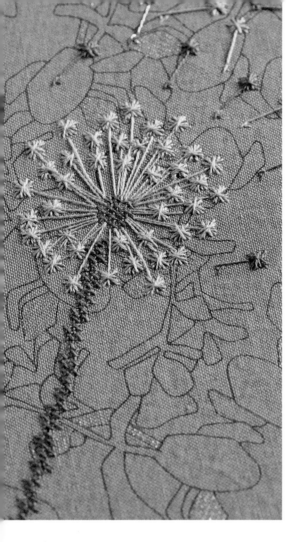

FROM TINY SEEDS...

These two little projects (see photo, page 81) provide a great excuse to go hunting through those vintage fabric stashes at the best markets. You can stitch these natural motifs onto anything you fancy and pick floss (thread) colors to match or contrast depending on your mood.

1 Prepare your fabric and position your soluble canvas, following the instructions on page 16.

2 Cross stitch the pattern onto your fabric as you would with normal aida, using the grid in the canvas.

3 Again following the instructions on page 17, rinse away the canvas and finish with a second piece of interfacing.

4 Paint the outer ring of the embroidery hoops in your chosen metallic color, then leave to dry. Frame your embroidery in the hoop (see page 18 for full instructions).

PATTERN SKILL LEVEL

ⅩⅩⅩⅩⅩ

MATERIAL SKILL LEVEL

ⅩⅩⅩⅩⅩ

YOU WILL NEED

For the dandelion puff
Chart on page 79

7⅞ x 7⅞ in. (20 x 20 cm) fabric of your choice (high-quality cotton and thin denim work particularly well)

5⅛ x 6 in. (13 x 15 cm) iron-on interfacing in a weight to match your fabric

5⅛ x 6 in. (13 x 15 cm) piece of DMC soluble canvas

DMC stranded cotton embroidery floss (thread) in the following colors: 3809 (dark turquoise), 597 (mid turquoise), E334 (metallic turquoise)

One 5-in. (12.5-cm) embroidery hoop

For the oak leaf and acorn
Chart on page 80

7⅞ x 9¾ in. (20 x 25 cm) fabric of your choice (high-quality cotton and thin denim work particularly well)

4½ x 7 in. (12 x 18 cm) iron-on interfacing in a weight to match your fabric

4½ x 7 in. (12 x 18 cm) piece of DMC soluble canvas

DMC stranded cotton embroidery floss (thread) in the following colors: 3820 (mustard), 167 (mid brown), 869 (dark brown)

Kreinik #004 very fine metallic thread in 002J (gold)

One 6-in. (15-cm) embroidery hoop

For both
Embroidery needle, size 4

Metallic acrylic paint in a tone to match your fabric

Paintbrush

Basic kit (see page 8)

FINISHED DESIGN SIZE

Dandelion puff: 4½ x 5⅛ in. (11.5 x 13 cm); 62 x 72 stitches

Oak leaf and acorn: 4 x 6 in. (10 x 15 cm); 56 x 83 stitches

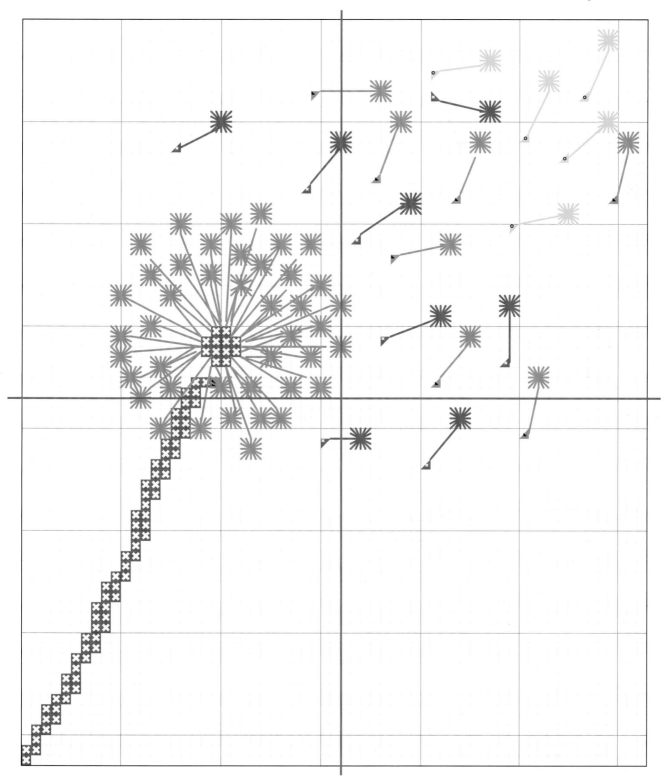

Thread color key for the dandelion puff

Symbol	DMC No	Description	Number of strands for cross stitch	Number of strands for long stitch
☒	3809	Dark turquoise	1	1
◣	597	Mid turquoise	1	1
◉	E334	Metallic turquoise	1	1

TANGLE ALERT

When using the metallic thread, keep the lengths much shorter than when using normal floss as it can tangle and fray more easily.

Thread color key for the oak leaf and acorn

Symbol	DMC No	Description	Number of strands for cross stitch	Number of strands for backstitch
▣	3820	Mustard	1	—
■	3820	Mustard	2	—
✖	167	Mid brown	1	—
◉	869	Dark brown	1	—

Symbol	Kreinik #004 very fine	Description	Number of strands for cross stitch	Number of strands for backstitch
▱	002J	Gold	—	1

FADING FLOWER TOTE

OK, I'll admit it—it may not be everyone's cup of tea to sit a bit awkwardly and stitch into a bag. But I found this great fun and the result has been admired on many a shopping trip since.

1 Use a tape measure to find the center point of the front of the bag and mark it with your needle. This shows you where to begin your stitching.

2 Find the center of the pattern indicated by the yellow lines on the chart on page 85. Working from the center outward and following the chart, stitch the flower motif (see pages 12–13), stitching into the grid of the burlap (jute) in just the same way as you would onto aida.

3 And the best bit is... no finishing required! The moment you've finished stitching, your bag is ready to use!

PATTERN SKILL LEVEL
✗ ✗ ✗ ✗ ✗

MATERIAL SKILL LEVEL
✗ ✗ ✗ ✗

YOU WILL NEED
Chart on page 85

Burlap (jute) bag (body measuring at least
12 x 12 in./30 x 30 cm)

DMC stranded cotton embroidery floss (thread) in
the following colors: B5200 (white), 3607 (bright pink),
211 (light violet), 153 (violet), 554 (dark violet),
553 (very dark violet), 3747 (light blue), 159 (blue),
156 (dark blue), 3838 (very dark blue)

Tapestry needle, size 22

Basic kit (see page 8)

FINISHED DESIGN SIZE
7 in. (18 cm) square; 84 x 90 stitches

TOP TIP
If you choose a laminated bag (where the inside is coated in a very thin layer of plastic), it will help to keep the bag in shape around your stitches. Use your needle to punch through the plastic with each stitch, gently removing any excess that comes away.

Thread color key

Symbol	DMC No	Description	Number of strands for cross stitch
⊘	B5200	White	2
✖	3607	Bright pink	2
⊙	211	Light violet	2
◖	153	Violet	2
●	554	Dark violet	2
◉	553	Very dark violet	2
▢	3747	Light blue	2
▣	159	Blue	2
◪	156	Dark blue	2
◼	3838	Very dark blue	2

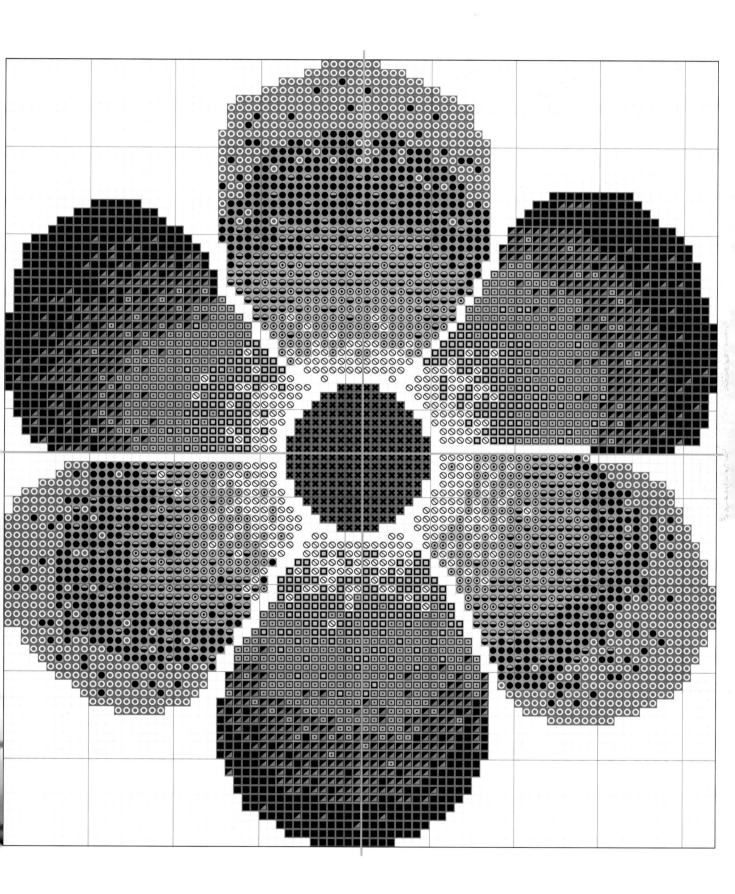

FLORAL FiNCH

This beautiful design looks intricate and difficult, but don't be put off. Take away the petal outlines and it is just blocks of solid color—easy to stitch, but so impressive.

The pattern is divided into four parts—left, right, top, and bottom —see diagram, right. Follow the center lines in yellow and the overlap sections to see how the four pieces fit together.

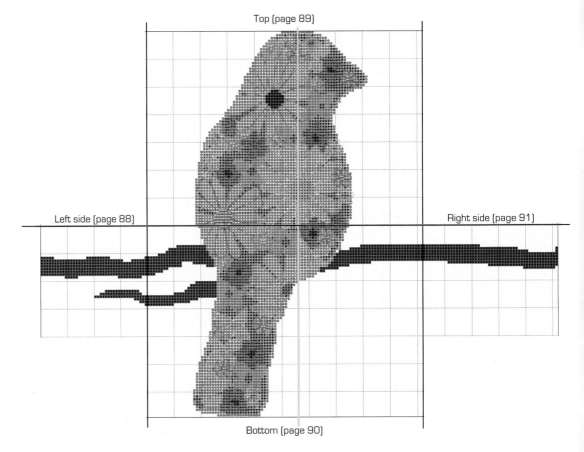

Top (page 89)

Left side (page 88)

Right side (page 91)

Bottom (page 90)

PATTERN SKILL LEVEL
✗ ✗ ✗ ✗ ✗

MATERIAL SKILL LEVEL
✗ ✗ ✗ ✗ ✗

YOU WILL NEED
Charts on pages 88–91

18-in. (45-cm) square of DMC 28-count linen in color 842

Two 14¾ x 9½-in. (37 x 24-cm) pieces of backing fabric for the back of the cover

DMC stranded cotton embroidery floss (thread) in the following colors: B5200 (white), ECRU (cream), 543 (beige), 3782 (mocha), 725 (yellow), 741 (tangerine), 894 (pink), 208 (purple), 3846 (turquoise), 995 (electric blue), 943 (bright green), 966 (light green), 720 (burnt orange)

Tapestry needle, size 26

14-in. (35-cm) pillow form (cushion pad)

Basic kit (see page 8)

FINISHED DESIGN SIZE
14 x 10 in. (35 x 25.5 cm); 193 x 137 stitches

1 Fold the linen in half across the length and width, and crease it. The point where the creases cross is the center of your fabric.

2 Find the center of the pattern, as indicated by the lines on the chart on page 89. Working from the center outward and following the chart, stitch the finch motif (see pages 12–13).

3 Make up the pillow (cushion) cover, following the instructions on pages 21–22. Insert a 14-in. (35-cm) pillow form (cushion pad).

Thread color key

Symbol	DMC No	Description	Number of strands for cross stitch	Number of strands for long stitch
◎	B5200	White	2	—
◉	ECRU	Cream	2	—
⊘	543	Beige	2	—
◓	3782	Mocha	2	—
◀	725	Yellow	2	1
▲	741	Tangerine	2	1
⬀	894	Pink	2	1
⋈	208	Purple	2	1
♥	3846	Turquoise	2	1
■	995	Electric blue	2	1
◪	943	Bright green	2	1
✳	966	Light green	2	—
✖	720	Burnt orange	2	—

Left side of floral finch — overlap

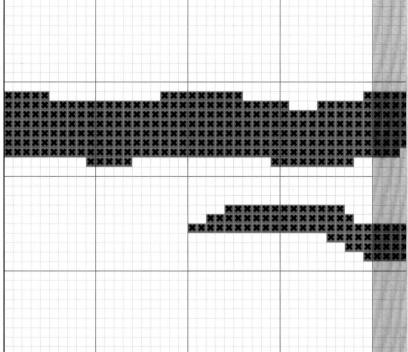

TOP TIP

Use long stitch rather than short backstitch around the petals to give a more rounded effect.

overlap

THIS WAY UP

Bottom of floral finch

THIS WAY UP

Thread color key

Symbol	DMC No	Description	Number of strands for cross stitch	Number of strands for long stitch
O	B5200	White	2	–
⊙	ECRU	Cream	2	–
⊘	543	Beige	2	–
●	3782	Mocha	2	–
◀	725	Yellow	2	1
▲	741	Tangerine	2	1
↗	894	Pink	2	1
⋈	208	Purple	2	1
♥	3846	Turquoise	2	1
■	995	Electric blue	2	1
◨	943	Bright green	2	1
✱	966	Light green	2	–
✸	720	Burnt orange	2	–

overlap

Right side of floral finch

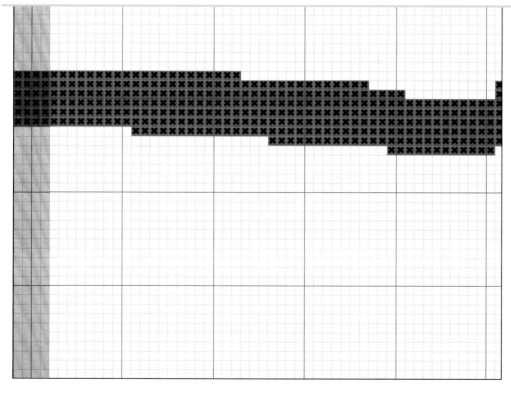

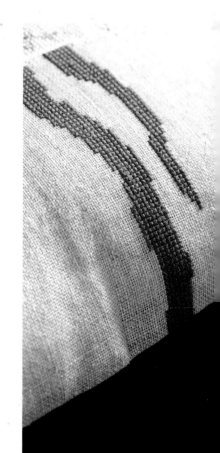

×××××××××××××××××××××××××××××

PATTERN SKILL LEVEL
× × × × ×

MATERIAL SKILL LEVEL
× × × × ×

YOU WILL NEED

Charts on pages 93–96

Two 8-in. (20-cm) squares of DMC 14-count white aida for the ladybug and butterfly

One 10 x 8-in. (25 x 20-cm) piece of DMC 14-count white aida for the dragonfly

DMC stranded cotton embroidery floss (thread) in the following colors: B5200 (white), 3779 (light pink), 760 (pink), 3328 (light red), 347 (red), 815 (dark red), 162 (palest blue), 813 (very light blue), 827 (light blue), 826 (blue), 825 (dark blue), 824 (very dark blue), 964 (light green), 959 (green), 3849 (dark green), 3848 (very dark green)

Pearl cotton thread

Tapestry needle, size 24

Two frames with a 5-in. (12.5-cm) square aperture

One frame with a 7 x 5-in. (18 x 12.5-cm) aperture

Three pieces of acid-free foam board or card slightly smaller than each of the frames

Basic kit (see page 8)

FINISHED DESIGN SIZE

Dragonfly: 6 x 3¾ in. (15 x 9.5 cm); 81 x 52 stitches

Ladybug: 3½ x 3½ in. (9 x 9 cm); 47 x 48 stitches

Butterfly: 4 x 3½ in. (10 x 9 cm); 54 x 47 stitches

STITCHY BUGS

This geometric collection of insects makes a perfect marriage of nature and mathematics.

1 Fold each fabric piece in half across the length and width, and crease it. The point where the creases cross is the center of your fabric.

2 Find the center of the pattern, as indicated by the lines on the charts on pages 93–96. Working from the center outward and following the chart, stitch the bug motifs (see pages 12–13).

3 Mount the finished embroideries in picture frames (see page 20).

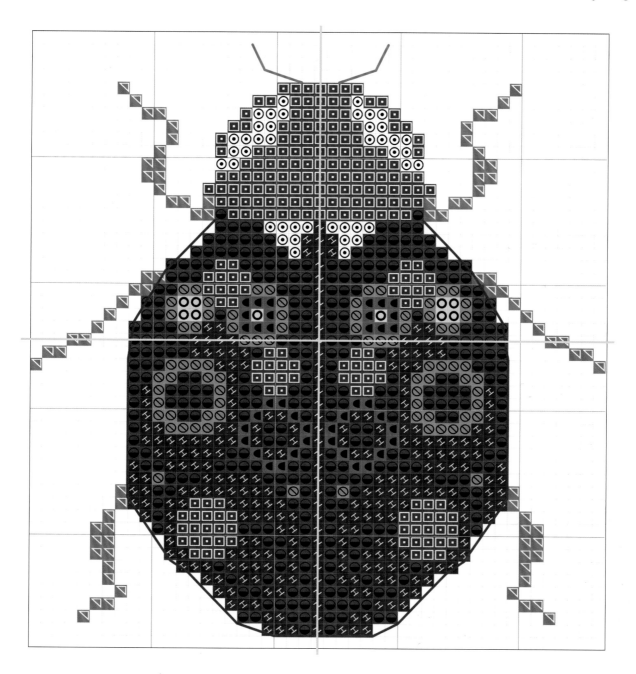

Thread color key for the ladybug

Symbol	DMC No	Description	Number of strands for cross stitch	Number of strands for long stitch
◉	B5200	White	2	—
◉	3779	Light pink	2	—
◎	760	Pink	2	—
◖	3328	Light red	2	—
●	347	Red	2	—
✦	815	Dark red	2	—
▣	824	Very dark blue	2	1
◣	3848	Very dark green	2	1

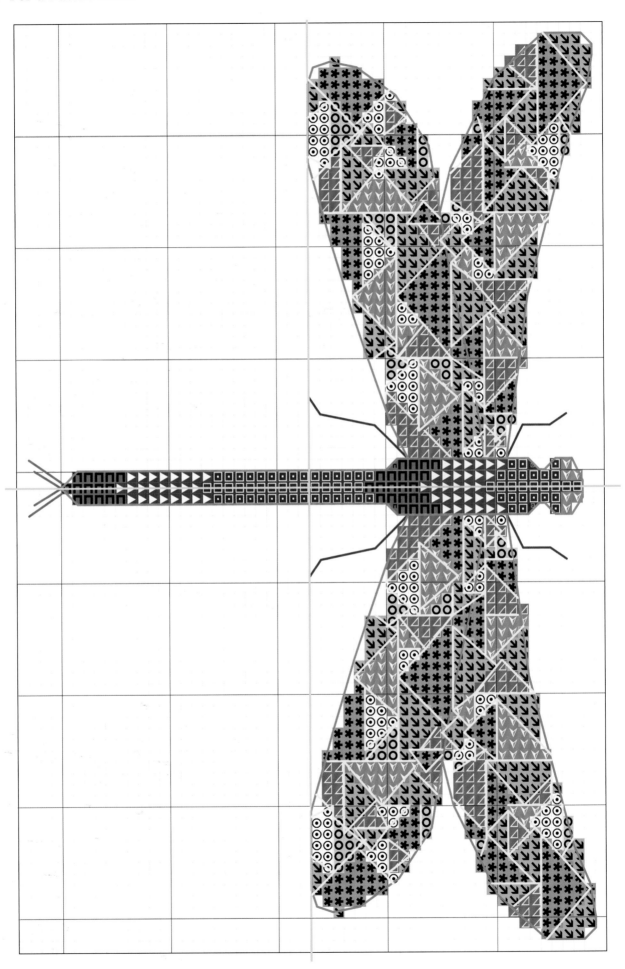

Thread color key for the dragonfly

Symbol	DMC No	Description	Number of strands for cross stitch	Number of strands for long stitch
⊙	B5200	White	2	—
◉	3779	Light pink	2	—
▣	827	Light blue	2	—
▲	826	Blue	2	—
▣	824	Very dark blue	2	1 (body)
↗	964	Light green	2	—
★	959	Green	2	—
▷	3849	Dark green	2	—
◥	3848	Very dark green	2	—
⊟	760	Pink	—	1 (wings)
▢	162	Palest blue	—	1 (wing veins)
⊟	347	Red	—	1 (legs)

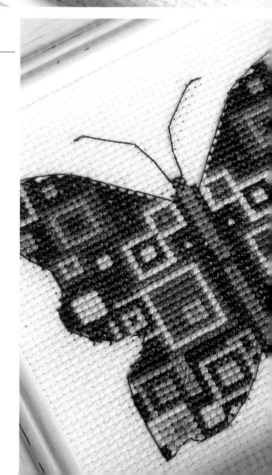

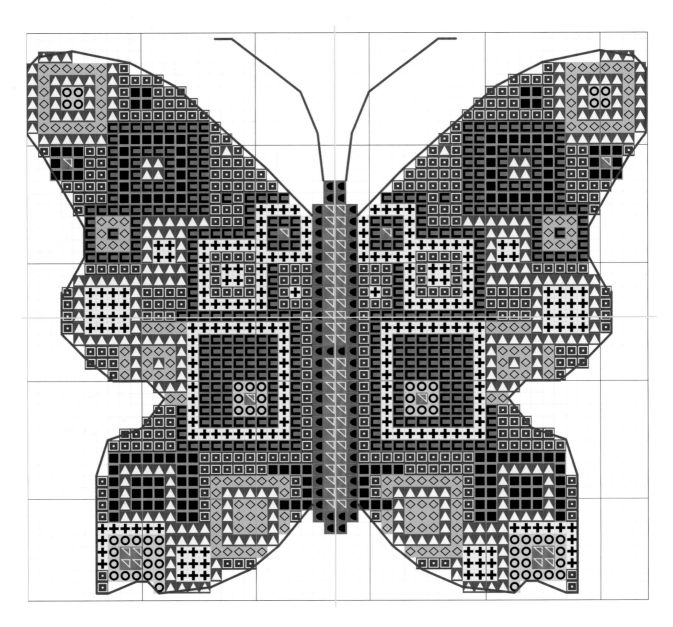

Thread color key for the butterfly

Symbol	DMC No	Description	Number of strands for cross stitch	Number of strands for long stitch
◙	3779	Light pink	2	—
◧	3328	Light red	2	1
➕	162	Palest blue	2	—
◇	813	Very light blue	2	—
▣	827	Light blue	2	—
△	826	Blue	2	—
■	825	Dark blue	2	—
▣	824	Very dark blue	2	—
◩	3848	Very dark green	2	—

PSYCHEDELIC RAINSTORM

I am convinced that this is actually how rainbows are made. The pretty colors against the silhouette make a lovely display and splitting the design across three hoops gives an extra twist of interest.

×××××××××××××××××××××××××××××××××××××

PATTERN SKILL LEVEL
× × × × ×

MATERIAL SKILL LEVEL
× × × × ×

YOU WILL NEED
Charts on pages 99–101

One 7-in. (18-cm) and two 8-in. (20-cm) squares of 28-count Zweigart Cashel linen in Smokey Pearl

Brightly colored felt backing fabric—one 5-in. (13-cm) and two 7-in. (18-cm) squares

DMC stranded cotton embroidery floss (thread) in the following colors: 310 (black), 517 (dark blue), 444 (yellow), 907 (green), 3846 (turquoise), 316 (dusty pink), 718 (bright pink), 3746 (purple)

Tapestry needle, size 26

Two 6-in. (15-cm) and one 4-in. (10-cm) wooden embroidery hoops

Acrylic paint in bright yellow

Paintbrush

Basic kit (see page 8)

FINISHED DESIGN SIZE
Rain cloud: 5 x 5 in. (13 x 13 cm); 69 x 69 stitches

Rain: 3¼ x 3½ in. (8 x 9 cm); 48 x 51 stitches

Sheltering girl: 3¼ x 5½ in. (8 x 14 cm); 46 x 78 stitches

1 Fold the linen pieces in half across the length and width, and crease them. The point where the creases cross is the center of your fabric.

2 Find the center of the pattern, as indicated by the lines on the charts on pages 99–101. Working from the center outward and following the charts, begin stitching (see pages 12–13).

3 Paint the outer ring of the embroidery hoops bright yellow, then leave them to dry. Frame your embroidery in the hoop (see page 18 for full instructions).

Thread color key for rain cloud

Symbol	DMC No	Description	Number of strands for cross stitch
◉	517	Dark blue	2
◀	444	Yellow	2
⊞	907	Green	2
▽	3846	Turquoise	2
↗	316	Dusty pink	2
✖	718	Bright pink	2
★	3746	Purple	2

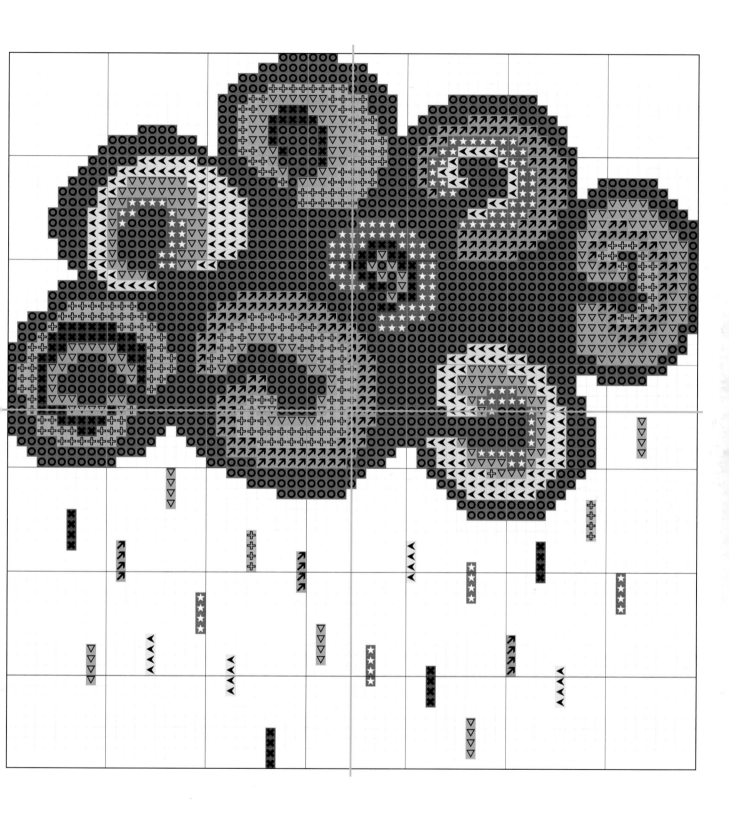

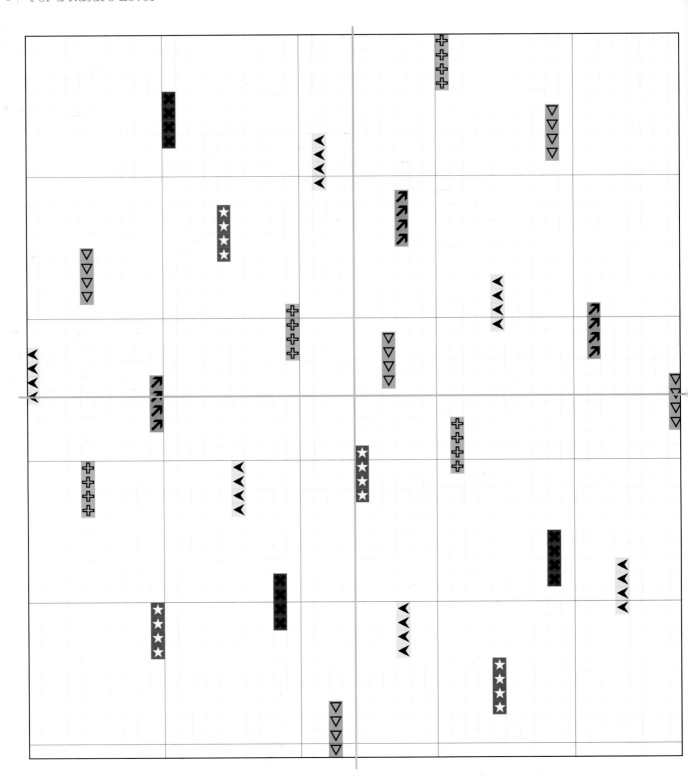

TOP TIP

There's no need to worry if you miscount a few squares here and there in the middle rain piece. No one will notice, I promise!

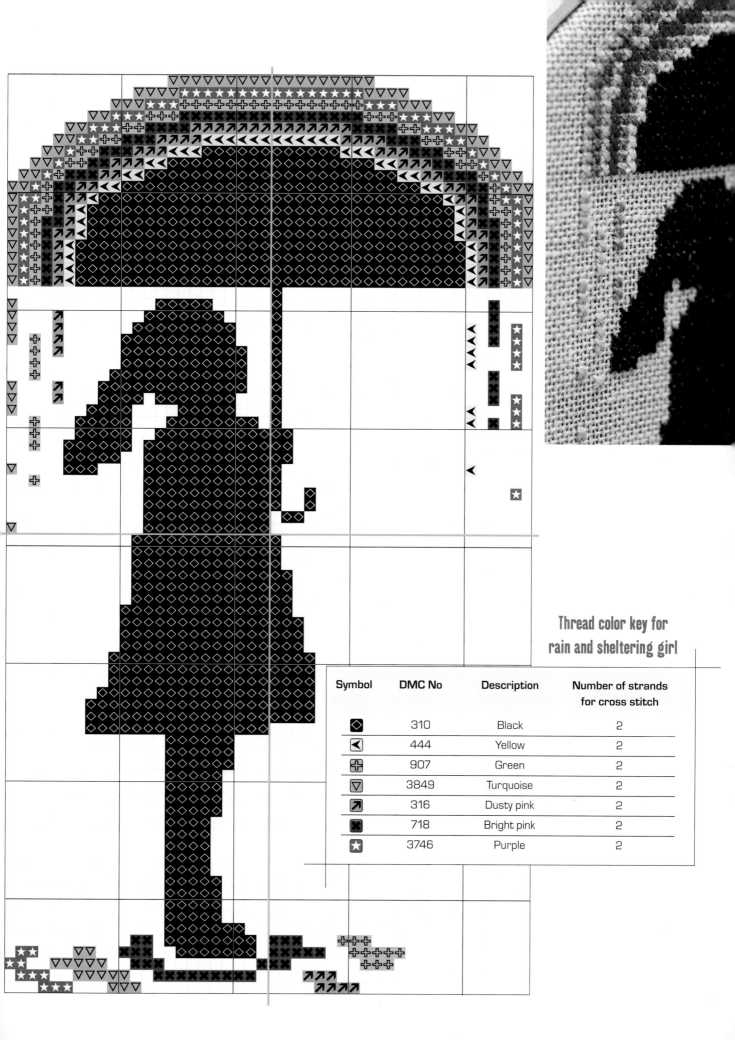

Thread color key for rain and sheltering girl

Symbol	DMC No	Description	Number of strands for cross stitch
◇	310	Black	2
◀	444	Yellow	2
✛	907	Green	2
▽	3849	Turquoise	2
↗	316	Dusty pink	2
✖	718	Bright pink	2
★	3746	Purple	2

FOR THE HOME

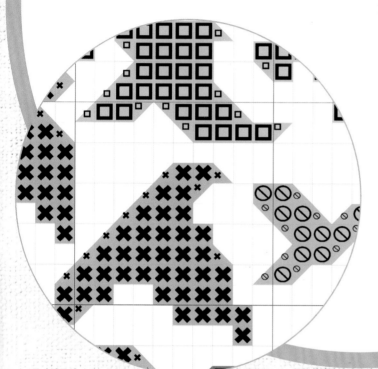

Let's face it—if you are going to make something to show off in your home, you want it to be marvelous. Then, when your friends admire it, you can casually beam and reply, "I made that." So this collection of rather fabulous projects should fit the bill.

GOLDFiSH BOWL

This pretty goldfish makes a perfect starter pet—no cleaning or feeding required, but still so pretty!

xxxxxxxxxxxxxxxxxxxxxxx

PATTERN SKILL LEVEL
✖ ✖ ✖ ✖ ✖

MATERIAL SKILL LEVEL
✖ ✖ ✖ ✖ ✖

YOU WILL NEED

Chart on page 106

16-in. (40-cm) square of 28-count Zweigart Cashel linen in Blue Spruce

12-in. (30-cm) square of backing fabric

DMC stranded cotton embroidery floss (thread) in the following colors: 3820 (light gold), 783 (dark gold), 722 (light peach), 922 (dark peach), 720 (burnt orange), 946 (bright orange), 900 (blood orange), 920 (amber), 310 (black)

Kreinik #004 very fine metallic threads in the following colors: 002J (gold), 152V (bronze), 1 (silver)

Tapestry needle, size 26

10-in. (25-cm) embroidery hoop

Silver acrylic paint

Paintbrush

Basic kit (see page 8)

FINISHED DESIGN SIZE

6¾ x 3½ in. (17 x 9 cm); 93 x 50 stitches

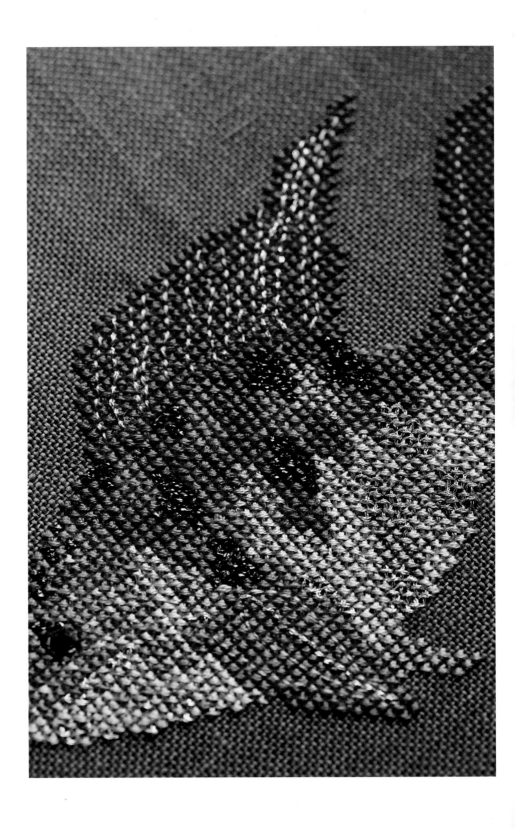

1 Fold the linen in half across the length and width, and crease it. The point where the creases cross is the center of your fabric.

2 Find the center of the pattern, as indicated by the lines on the chart on page 106. Working from the center outward and following the chart, stitch the goldfish motif (see pages 12–13).

3 Paint the outer ring of the embroidery hoop silver, then leave it to dry. Frame your embroidery in the hoop (see page 18 for full instructions).

TOP TIP

There are a lot of similar shades of orange here. Separate out your thread colors before you start, and make sure they stay clearly labeled throughout to avoid confusion.

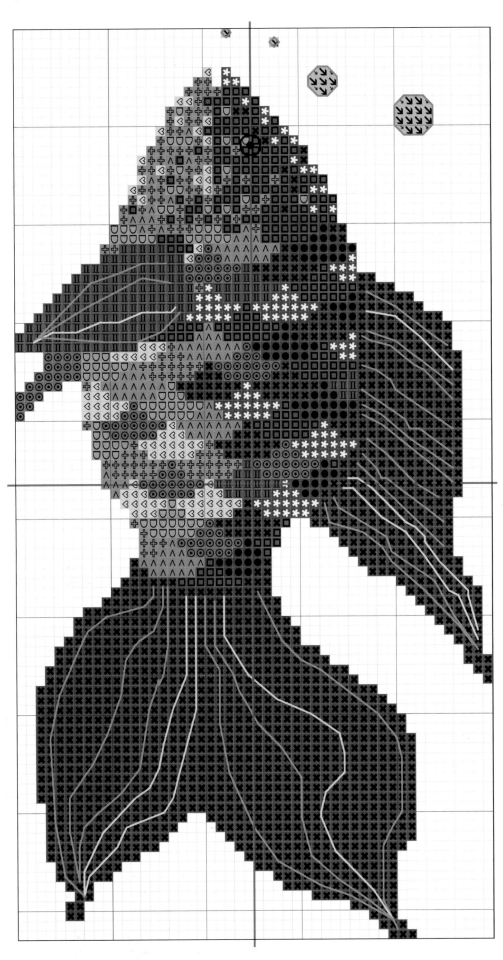

Thread color key

Symbol	DMC No	Description	Number of strands for cross stitch	Number of strands for backstitch
D	3820	Light gold	2	1
✛	783	Dark gold	2	—
<	722	Light peach	2	—
◉	922	Dark peach	2	—
▬	720	Burnt orange	2	—
◘	946	Bright orange	2	—
✖	900	Blood orange	2	—
●	920	Amber	2	—
▬	310	Black	—	2

Symbol	Krenik #004 very fine	Description	Number of strands for cross stitch	Number of strands for backstitch
♡	002J	Gold	1	1
✹	152V	Bronze	1	—
↗	1	Silver	1	1

TANGLE ALERT

Use two strands of black floss for the French knot center of the fish eye (see page 14).

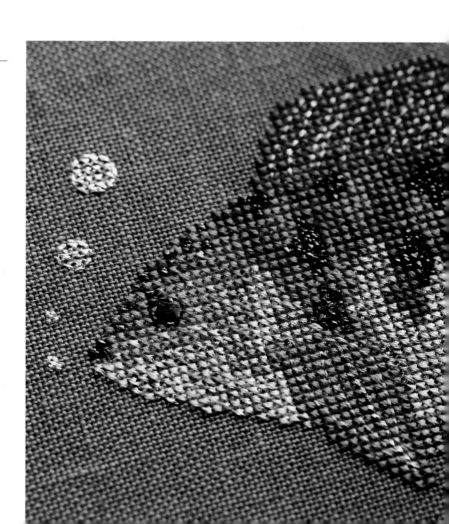

EXPLODING HEARTS

When I designed this, I pictured those old-fashioned cartoons where the lead character sees the love of their life for the first time and hearts explode from every pore. I imagine this is what their heart might look like. You can either display all three hearts together as a sequence, as I have done, or stitch just one for a romantic display.

PATTERN SKILL LEVEL
✗ ✗ ✗ ✗ ✗

MATERIAL SKILL LEVEL
✗ ✗ ✗ ✗ ✗

YOU WILL NEED

Charts on pages 10–11

Three 8-in. (20-cm) squares of 14-count white aida

Three 4¾-in. (12-cm) pieces of backing fabric

DMC stranded cotton embroidery floss (thread) in the following colors: 891 (dark pink), 894 (light pink), 964 (mint)

Tapestry needle, size 24

Three 4-in. (10-cm) embroidery hoops

Silver acrylic paint

Paintbrush

Basic kit (see page 8)

FINISHED DESIGN SIZE OF LARGEST PIECE

3⅛ x 3⅛ in. (8 x 8 cm); 44 x 42 stitches

1 Fold each piece of aida fabric in half across the length and width, and crease it. The point where the creases cross is the center of your fabric.

2 Find the center of each pattern, as indicated by the lines on the charts on pages 110–111. Working from the center outward and following the chart, stitch the heart motifs (see pages 12–13).

3 Paint the outer rings of the embroidery hoops silver, then leave them to dry. Frame your embroidery in the hoops (see page 18 for full instructions).

TANGLE ALERT

In the final exploded heart (on page 110), the short backstitch lines represent quarter stitches (see page 15).

Thread color key

Symbol	DMC No	Description	Number of strands for cross stitch	Number of strands for backstitch
✖	891	Dark pink	2	1
◉	894	Light pink	2	—
▣	964	Mint	2	1

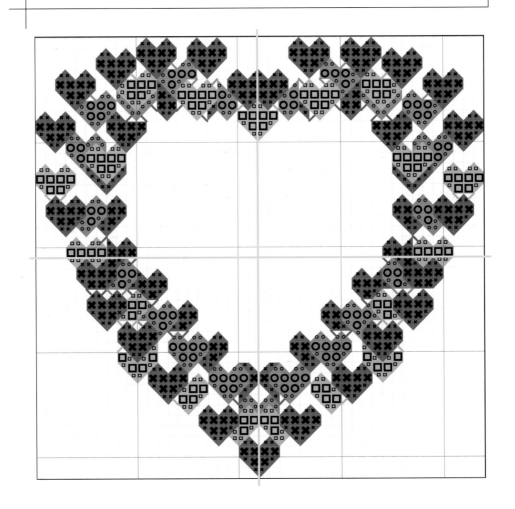

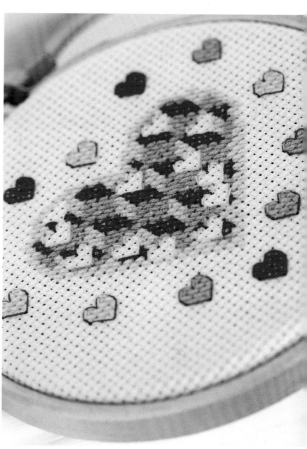

WASHI-TAPE WALL BIRDS

Washi tape—a decorative tape from Japan—is a wonderful invention. Widely available in good craft stores, it comes in loads of colors and patterns and in a range of different widths. Using it to "cross stitch" like this is an affordable and easy way of keeping your interiors scheme up to date. It can be removed easily without leaving a mark, so you can change the picture with the seasons and stay completely on trend.

X X X X X X X X X X X X X X X X X X X X X X X X X X X X X X X X X X X

PATTERN SKILL LEVEL
✕ ✕ ✕ ✕ ✕

MATERIAL SKILL LEVEL
✕ ✕ ✕ ✕ ✕

YOU WILL NEED

Chart on page 114

Washi tape ⁵⁄₈ in. (15 mm) wide—two 11-yd (10-m) rolls each of dark turquoise, lilac, and light turquoise; one 11-yd (10-m) roll each of silver and bright pink

Long ruler

Sharp pencil

Spirit level

Paper scissors

Eraser

FINISHED DESIGN SIZE

52½ x 63 in. (140 x 168 cm); 35 x 42 stitches

1 Using a pencil and a long ruler, lightly draw a rectangle on the wall measuring 52½ in. wide x 63 in. tall (140 x 168 cm). Use the spirit level to make sure your horizontal and vertical lines are straight. Mark off lines at 1½-in. (4-cm) intervals across and down to create a grid to show you where each "stitch" should go.

2 Following the pattern, just as you would with regular cross stitch, cut or tear 2-in. (5-cm) lengths of the tape and stick them in little crosses in the appropriate square (see Top Tip, right). In this way, you will get 100 "stitches" from each roll of tape.

3 Once you have finished, erase any pencil marks that are still visible.

X X X X X X X X X X X X X X X X X X X X X X X X X X X X X X X X X X X X

TOP TIP

You can tear your tape as I did for a more rustic "sewn" look or cut it with scissors for a neater finish.

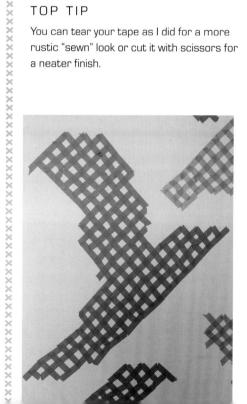

Thread color key

Symbol	Washi tape width	Description
■	⅝ in. (15 mm)	Dark turquoise
✖	⅝ in. (15 mm)	Lilac
▢	⅝ in. (15 mm)	Light turquoise
⊘	⅝ in. (15 mm)	Silver
◣	⅝ in. (15 mm)	Bright pink

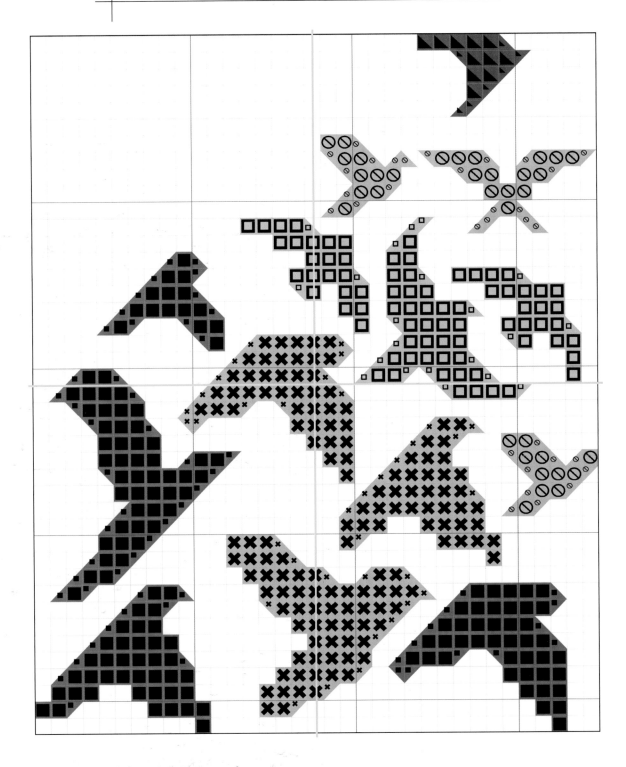

TAKE A SEAT

This project was a complete pleasure from start to finish. The velvet ribbon gives a beautifully sumptuous finish and is so tactile—I couldn't stop stroking it! The two-color design can be adapted to match your own color scheme. For a great vintage finish, paint the edge of the woven seat base with gold acrylic paint and leave it to dry for 24 hours before you start to stitch.

xxxxxxxxxxxxxxxxxxxxxxxxx

PATTERN SKILL LEVEL
x x x x x

MATERIAL SKILL LEVEL
x x x x x

YOU WILL NEED

Chart on page 116

44 yd (40 m) velvet ribbon, ¼ in. (7 mm) wide, in each of two colors

Tapestry needle, size 16

Gold acrylic paint

Paintbrush

Basic kit (see page 8)

FINISHED DESIGN SIZE

10 ¾ in. (27.5 cm) long x 12 in. (30 cm) at widest point, narrowing to 9½ in. (24 cm); 22 x 20 stitches

Thread color key

Symbol	Thread	Description	Number of strands for cross stitch
⊙	Velvet ribbon, ¼ in. (7 mm) wide	Burgundy/gold	1
✖	Velvet ribbon, ¼ in. (7 mm) wide	Gold/burgundy	1

1 Find a pair of chairs with a woven cane seat base. Try to make sure that the grid created by the weave is as even as possible. Also make sure that the holes in the grid are big enough to fit your ribbon.

2 Paint a 2-in. (5-cm) strip of the outer edges of the cane seat base with one coat of gold acrylic paint and leave to dry for 24 hours. (There is no need to paint the whole base, as most of it will be covered with your stitches.)

3 Cut a 1- or 2-yd (1- or 2-m) length of ribbon and thread your needle.

4 Stitch into the base of your seat as you would onto aida, stitching into every square of the cane weave "grid." Take care to catch the ribbon

underneath the first few stitches to secure it, as described on page 12. You can turn the chair upside down if that helps.

5 Try to stitch right up to the edge of the seat base, although this does get more difficult as you get closer to where the cane is secured to the wood. Stitch as close to the edge as you possibly can.

6 Finish each length of ribbon in the same way as you would with floss (thread), by turning the chair upside down and passing your needle underneath the back of a few stitches to secure the ribbon.

7 Once you have finished your stitching, simply stand back and admire!

TOP TIPS

- If your chairs are larger than the ones I used, just continue the base color until you reach the edge.

- Try using leather or faux suede cord or chunky tapestry yarn to give a different look and texture.

xxxxxxxxxxxxxxxxxxxxxxxxxxxxxxxxxx

PATTERN SKILL LEVEL
x x x x

MATERIAL SKILL LEVEL
x x x x x

YOU WILL NEED

Chart on page 119

DMC stranded cotton embroidery floss (thread) in the following colors: 336 (dark blue), 601 (bright pink)

DMC light effects floss (thread) in E415 (metallic silver)

Embroidery needle, size 4

One ½ x 1¾-in. (12 x 45-mm) pre-perforated wooden pendant

Key ring

Basic kit (see page 8)

FINISHED DESIGN SIZE

½ x 1½ in. (1.2 x 4-cm); 6 x 21 stitches

LIGHT AS A FEATHER

This pretty and simple feather is stitched in three bold colors with a hint of shine. Using a gorgeous pre-punched wooden pendant (widely available on the internet) is a great way to make a key ring and a perfect way to show off your stitching skills. If your pendant is a little bigger than this one, the design is easy to adapt to make a little wider or longer.

1 Measure or count to find the center of your wooden pendant. Following the chart, stitch your design. Secure your thread in the same way that you would on normal aida, by catching the end under the initial few stitches. Finish off in the same way, too, by pushing your needle underneath the back of some finished stitches. If you are worried about the back of your stitching looking untidy, glue a small piece of felt over the top to cover it up.

2 Insert a metal key ring through the large hole at the top of the pendant.

xxxxxxxxxxxxxxxxxxxxxxxxxxxxxxx
x
x   TOP TIP
x
x   You might want to use a thimble here,
x   otherwise you risk pricking your finger
x   if you miss the holes!
x

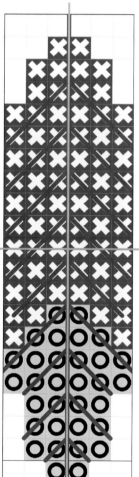

Thread color key

Symbol	DMC No	Description	Number of strands for cross stitch	Number of strands for long stitch
☒	336	Dark blue	1	—
◉	E415	Metallic silver	1	—
⊟	601	Bright pink	—	1

TARTAN DACHSHUND

XXXXXXXXXXXXXXXXXXXXXXXXXX

PATTERN SKILL LEVEL
X X X X X

MATERIAL SKILL LEVEL
X X X X X

YOU WILL NEED
Charts on pages 122–124

16 x 22-in. (40 x 56-cm) piece of
28-count DMC linen (color 842)

Two 12½-in. (32-cm) squares of
backing fabric of your choice

DMC stranded cotton embroidery
floss (thread) in the following colors:
312 (dark blue), 817 (red),
3820 (yellow), 3865 (white),
519 (light blue)

Tapestry needle, size 26

12 x 18-in. (30 x 45-cm) pillow form
(cushion pad)

Basic kit (see page 8)

FINISHED DESIGN SIZE
12¾ x 7¼ in. (32.5 x 18.5 cm);
178 x 101 stitches

Your finished pillow (cushion) will
measure 12 x 18 in. (30 x 45 cm)

The tartan design in our low-slung friend is beautiful,
but a challenge. To get that classic woven tartan effect,
this pattern contains lots of combined stitches (the
bottom half-stitch in one color, the top half-stitch in
another). So, if you're ready, thread up and dive in.

1 Take a look at your pattern. Squares in a
pattern that are split into triangles like this
(see below left) usually mean three-quarter
stitches. Not this time! Instead, the square should
be stitched in half-stitches (see page 12) of two
colors. (At the time of writing, I couldn't find an
official term for this stitch—so for now, let's
christen it a Bobo stitch!)

Top triangle =
lightest color =
top half-stitch;
bottom triangle =
darkest color =
bottom half-stitch

2 To keep everything neat and tidy, you need to
make sure all of your bottom and top stitches
lie in the same direction (no matter what the color).

The darker color is always your bottom stitch.
To help you, the pattern shows the darker color
in the bottom triangle and the light color in the
top triangle.

As an example, the white thread will only ever
be in the direction of your top stitch, as the lightest
color. The dark blue will only ever be in the
direction of your bottom stitch as it is the darkest
color. Red and yellow stitches could be either
direction depending on the color they are paired
with. Our key shows the paired colors in order,
from darkest at the top to lightest at the bottom.
(The light blue is only ever used on its own, not in
combination with another color.)

Say you have navy blue and red in the same
square. If you've decided your bottom stitches will
always run from bottom left to top right, you
should work the navy blue half-stitch from bottom
left to top right, and red half-stitch from bottom

right to top left. However, if you have red and white in the same square, the red is the darker color—so that's the one you work from bottom left to top right.

3 When you have finished stitching the Dachshund, trim your fabric down to 18½ x 12½ in. (47 x 32 cm), taking care to keep the design in the center. Make up the cover, following the instructions on pages 21–22.

the instructions on pages 21–22.

TOP TIP

Stitch in sections, one color at a time. Start with navy, then red, then yellow, then white. This will prompt you as to which color should be your bottom stitch (see step 2).

This pattern is divided into three parts: the left, center, and right—see diagram, right. Follow the center lines in yellow and the overlap sections to see how the three pieces fit together.

Left side (below)   Center (opposite page)   Right side (page 124)

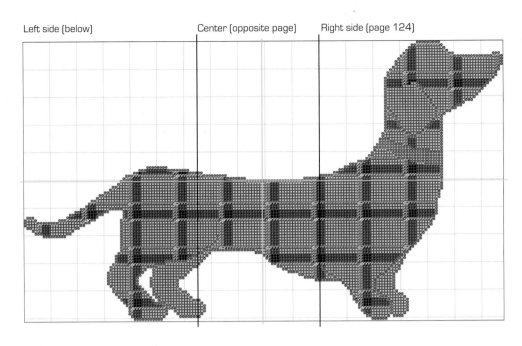

Left side of Tartan Dachshund

overlap

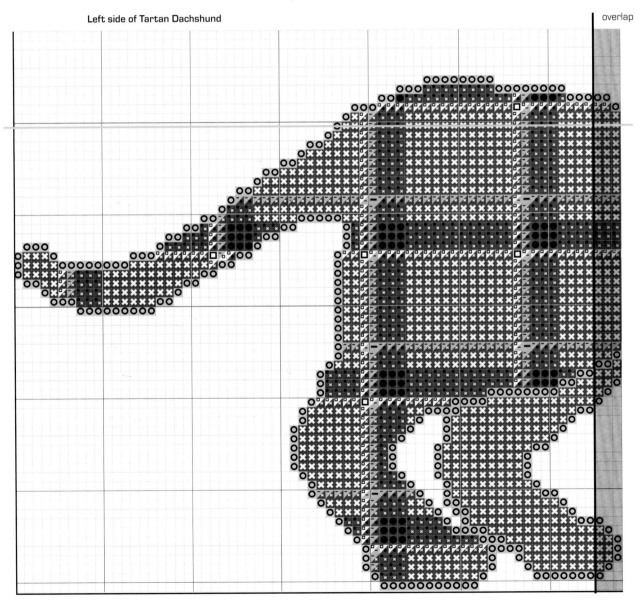

Thread color key

Symbol	DMC No	Description	Number of strands for cross stitch
☒	312	Navy blue	2
●	817	Red	2
⊟	3820	Yellow	2
☐	3865	White	2
◉	519	Light blue	2

Center of Tartan Dachshund

overlap

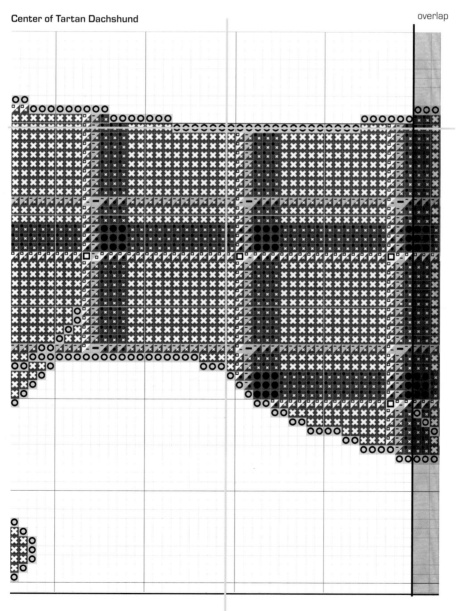

Right side of Tartan Dachshund

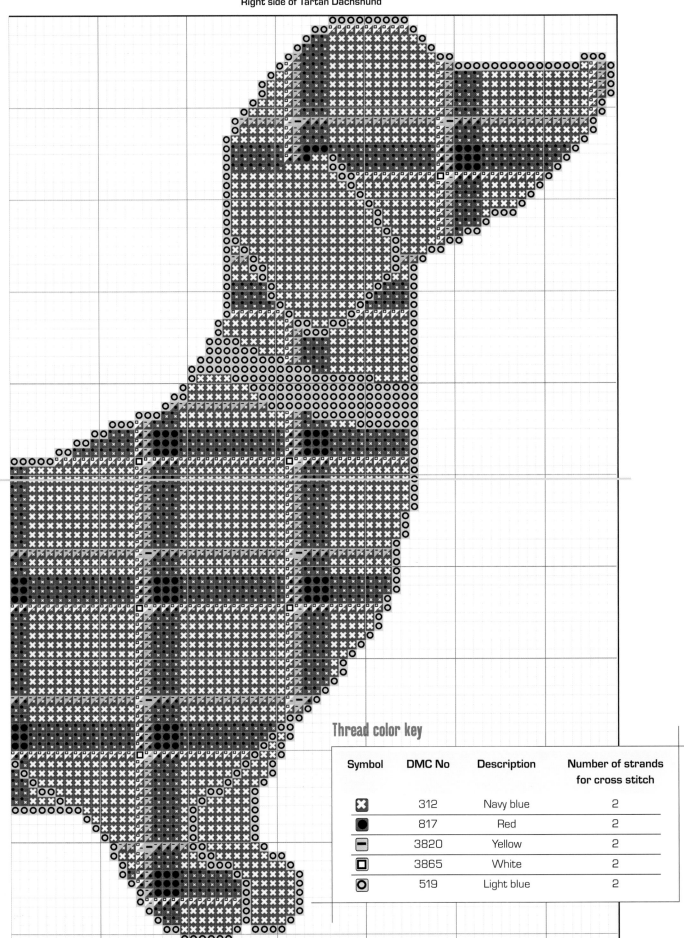

Thread color key

Symbol	DMC No	Description	Number of strands for cross stitch
❌	312	Navy blue	2
⬤	817	Red	2
⊟	3820	Yellow	2
⊡	3865	White	2
◉	519	Light blue	2

SUPPLIERS

AUTHOR'S WEBSITE

Bobo Stitch
This is my very own website, where you can buy all my cross-stitch kits. I ship globally.
www.bobostitch.co.uk

MANUFACTURERS

DMC Creative World
Buy DMC threads online or find details of your local stockist.
www.dmc-usa.com or
www.dmccreative.co.uk

Kreinik
Buy Kreinik threads online or find details of your local stockist.
Tel: 1-800-537-2166 or
1-304-422-8900
www.kreinik.com

GENERAL ONLINE SUPPLIERS

Amazon
Great for all kinds of things, from fabric and threads to unusual things to stitch onto, such as the iPhone case on page 42.
www.amazon.co.uk and
www.amazon.com

Etsy
A good source of craft supplies and fabric. I bought the wooden pendant on page 118 from Beadeux.
www.etsy.com/uk/shop/Beadeux

US SUPPLIERS

1-2-3 Stitch!
Tel: 1-800-996-1230
www.123stitch.com

Fabricville
Over 170 stores in Canada.
www.fabricville.com

Hobby Lobby
Stores nationwide.
www.hobbylobby.com

Jo-Ann Fabric and Craft Store
Stores nationwide.
Tel: 1-888-739-4120
www.joann.com

Michaels
Stores nationwide.
Tel: 1-800-642-4235
www.michaels.com

Needle Travel
Listings of fiber and fabric stores.
www.needletravel.com

Yarn Tree
Tel: 800-247-3952 or
515-232-3121
www.yarntree.com

UK SUPPLIERS

Back Stitch
Gorgeous haberdashery.
Tel: 01223 778118
www.backstitch.co.uk

Cloud Craft
Fabric, threads, and wool felt.
www.cloudcraft.co.uk

Hobbycraft
Stores nationwide.
Tel: 0330 026 1400
www.hobbycraft.co.uk

I Love Cross Stitch
Everything you need for your favorite hobby.
Tel: 0844 880 5851
www.ilovecrossstitch.co.uk

John Lewis
Stores nationwide.
Tel: 08456 049 049
www.johnlewis.com

Sew and So
Tel: 0800 013 0150
www.sewandso.co.uk

Willow Fabrics
Tel: 0800 0567 811
www.willowfabrics.com

ACKNOWLEDGMENTS

Before I started this book, I always imagined writing to be quite a lonely process—shut up all day in an office with a view of a blossom tree, just you and a typewriter. OK, so it was quite an old-fashioned, quaint imagining, but I always thought of it as a solo enterprise. But this book really has been a hugely collective effort, so there are many people to whom I would like to express my gratitude in writing.

To Cindy from CICO. Thank you for spotting me and offering me the opportunity to write this book. It's been a blast, I've loved every minute. Your team, particularly Penny and Carmel, have been kind, encouraging, and willing to let my creativity lead the way, which has been invigorating and beautifully challenging.

I have been carried along on a tidal wave of enthusiasm and endless offers of gratefully received childcare by my girlfriends Louise, Sal, Whizz, Becky, Jenny, Hannah, Katie, and the rest of the gang. You guys rock—fact.

To my nana, who has provided lots of wonderful stitchy inspiration, my aunt Amanda, aunty Helen, and my mum for doing some sterling sample stitching.

To Ellen Mary. I love you, you are ace. Thank you for being my partner in crime, my business buddy, and an endless ray of sunshine.

To my wonderful in-laws, Bruce and Libby—you have, without complaint, put up with me descending on you during the holidays and then abandoning you with the kids for long periods of time. Thank you.

Ditto to my parents. Mum, Dad, you are amazing. So supportive in every way that I have ever needed. I love you and I hope that this book makes you half as proud of me as I am grateful to you.

To my husband, James, who is just the best. I cannot tell you how appreciative I am for everything. Thank you for not begrudging the neglect inflicted upon you for the duration. I do not have enough superlatives. So you know, Banana Pancakes and all that.

And to my babies, Wilf and Olive, who are ultimately my inspiration and have changed my life endlessly for the good.

Peeping Ted (page 29) alphabet charts

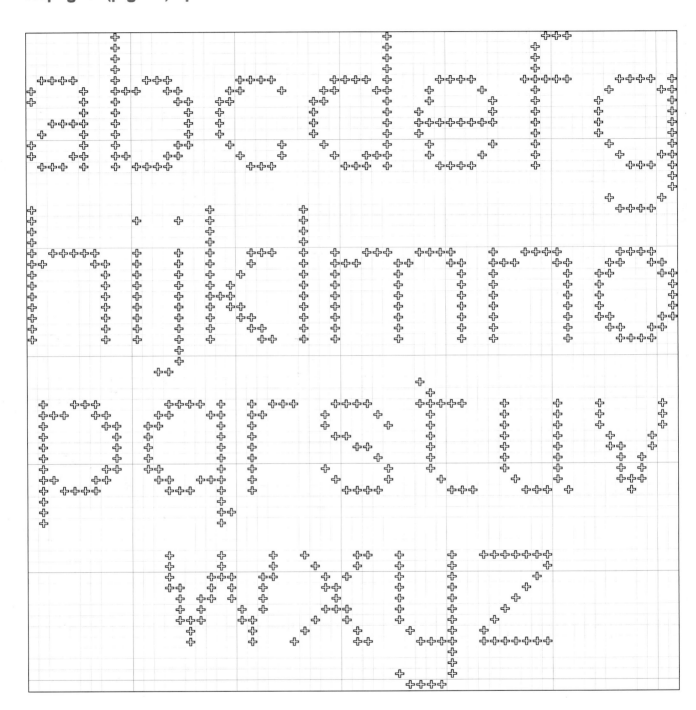

INDEX